Dedication

For Jordan and Andrew,

The bravest young men I know—who lifted me when I couldn't stand,
walked beside me as we found our way through grief and sorrow,
and reminded me, again and again, that love endures.

THERESA BRUNO

He's Not Coming Back

Rewriting Life after Loss: A Path to Healing

Published: April 2025

ISBN: 979-8-9926661-4-4

Library of Congress Control Number: 2025903924

For information address:
The Three Tomatoes Book Publishing
6 Soundview Rd.
Glen Cove, NY 11542

Cover design: Mary Pat McGlawn
Interior design: nycartdirector.com

This book is intended to provide helpful and informative material on the subjects addressed. It is not meant to replace the advice or services of healthcare professionals. The author and publisher specifically disclaim any responsibility for any liability, loss, or risk, personal or otherwise, which is incurred as a consequence, directly or indirectly, of the use and application of any of the contents of this book.

All product names, trademarks, and registered trademarks are property of their respective owners. Mention of these products and trademarks is for informational purposes only and does not imply endorsement or affiliation with the author or publisher.

Preface

This book was born from a season of profound loss and transformation. In the wake of my husband James' death, my world shattered, leaving me with questions that had no immediate answers. Grief reshaped me at my core, forcing me to confront who I was without James or the roles, definitions, and achievements I had spent my life building.

For the first time, I realized I had been telling myself stories—stories about what success should look like, who I needed to be, and how I was expected to move through the world. None of those stories fit anymore.

In the aftermath, I wasn't sure what I was looking for. All I knew was that I didn't want to live in a narrative of endless sorrow and hopelessness. Instead, I started searching for a way forward to rewrite my story and create a life that wasn't defined by what had happened to me and my family but held both my pain and the possibility of rebuilding.

That search became the foundation of this book.

There was no roadmap for the journey I found myself on. Closing my business, reimaging my life, and grappling with the weight of grief left me vulnerable in a way I had never known before. But in that vulnerability, I learned so much. I learned how to survive the initial, gut-wrenching early days of grief and sorrow; I found a bread-crumb trail of courage that showed up day after day, guiding me out of my abject grief. I learned that sharing my pain was essential to my healing. I leaned hard into trusted friendships and my children—who have been my anchors. And ultimately, I learned to dream again. It is not at all like I had dreamed before, but dreams born from suffering and seeing life through an entirely new lens.

I didn't write this book simply to share my story but with the hope that in its telling, anyone who has experienced profound loss, betrayal, sorrow, or grief might find a kindred spirit—someone who understands the depth of their pain. If I've learned one thing in my journey, it's that we are all surviving something.

I also hope that for those who have questioned how to pick up the pieces after life has brought them to their knees, or who are searching for the strength to go on when it feels like there's no path forward, that my story will give you strength and the assurance that moving forward is possible.

It's a book about survival, and it's a book about looking hard at life's most challenging questions. It's about finding meaning in the messy in-between parts and daring to imagine what's on the other side of sorrow and loss.

Throughout these pages, I will share the lessons I've learned and the truths I've uncovered. I will also share how I learned to listen to the stories I was telling myself and how I began to rewrite them.

This book is deeply personal, but it's not just for me. I hope these words remind you of your courage and give you the strength to keep going in your survival journey.

Thank you for being here with me and for reading. This story isn't over yet—not mine or yours.

Table of Contents

Chapter 1

An ordinary Saturday in April

I know that wishing is foolish, but if I could have one wish, I would wish that he had planted the sunflowers. Maybe then he would have reconsidered. Maybe then he would have stayed.

We had a little cottage on Smith Lake, about ninety miles north of Birmingham, Alabama. Tucked away at the end of a winding dirt road, our house was perched high on a rock cropping, offering a serene view of a quiet slew. We had to walk through a cave-like cut in the rocks to reach the water, a spiritual passage that always prompted me to reflect and offer gratitude.

Smith Lake is known for its clear, clean water and stunning shoreline. It was created when Alabama Power flooded the area to form a forty-mile-long lake, leaving tall trees standing and creating a deep lake with beautiful blue-green water. Nestled in a rural area surrounded by farmland with no organized housing development, it felt like time out of place for us.

There were so many unexpected experiences that charmed us. I am a classically trained pianist, and I mostly listen to classical music. Late one afternoon, as the sun began to set, I was listening to a Mozart concerto through a small speaker on our porch; I laughed out loud when, a few minutes into the concerto, Mozart was accompanied by the loud moos of cows coming in from a farm across the water. I was convinced they weren't just mooing as they came in for dinner; they were mooing in response to the music.

My husband, James, and I cherished that little cottage and the surrounding property. Tucked in the woods, with waterfalls, wild hydrangea, and mountain laurel, it was our sanctuary, a place that felt restorative and peaceful.

A long marriage always has times when it needs healing. When we bought that cottage, we knew we were on the precipice of a new place in our lives that needed time together and space to recharge.

My early life was not easy. Hoping to put salve on the pain of childhood abuse, I spent my life trying to create beauty— first as a musician, then as a creative partner in a marketing firm, followed by unexpected success as a jewelry designer.

Even though we had been married for over twenty years at that point, I had never shared much of my childhood with James. It was a dark place that I had pushed deep down, and in my mind, there was no point in sharing it. It was just too much for anyone else to bear. I've learned a lot about sharing my pain in recent years, but at that point, I was just beginning to let a little of it come to the surface.

James was going through a difficult time in his business, which smacked hard at his self-esteem. After his family sold their business, James struggled to find the success he had hoped for in the partnerships and businesses he pursued. He held his feelings closely, too, but I could see him beginning to shrink— from life, from me, from himself.

Our lives revolved around raising our boys, running businesses, and being active in our community. However, cracks began to show in our scaffolding. James seemed to carry a sense of unworthiness due to unmet dreams while I was dealing with enormous stress as my jewelry business struggled. I, too, was questioning my worth as a businessperson and a creative person.

Our little cottage became our refuge. I would spend days paddling on the lake, taking lazy afternoon naps, and enjoying the amazing meals James prepared. Every weekend was a culinary delight. Our cottage was secluded, with no nearby stores or restaurants. We often joked that whatever you wanted to eat, you had to bring with you. There was no alternative. James, who loved to cook, would spend days ahead of time thinking about how to create the best meals for us. We often spent late evenings by the fire pit, drinking wine, star gazing, and talking.

One weekend, a month into COVID, a week after Easter in 2020, we had plans to plant a sunflower garden at the lake. I was so excited about the idea of a beautiful, happy, yellow garden. My romantic daydreams of the sunflower fields Van Gogh painted were my inspiration, and I could already envision the big yellow flowers against the backdrop of the colors of the lake. Four large bags of sunflower seeds were in our garage, waiting to be planted.

After a long client meeting on Friday evening, I returned to our home in Birmingham, eager to talk to James about my day. I always talked through everything in my business with him. He had a clear business head and an intuition that was seldom wrong. I relied on his wisdom and guidance, both in business and in all of life. He was always steady and measured. He had an indomitable sense of humor that often balanced my serious nature and created a constant layer of fun.

When I arrived that evening, I noticed that he was different. He was quieter than usual, almost solemn. He didn't have his usual sense of witty humor and sarcasm. He was also drinking a mixed drink, which he never did unless we were entertaining. He always drank wine, and that only moderately.

In the weeks before April 19th, James seemed more down than usual. His anxiety often ran high, but in those weeks, he was more agitated than usual. He had been battling a low-level kind of depression for several years after the deaths of both his mother and his dad.

For the first time in our marriage, we were in therapy. We had been seeing a wise and wonderful therapist for about a year. Strangely, when I look back on that year, nothing came forward in therapy that was life-shattering, nothing so broken or egregiously wrong that it couldn't be worked on.

We were beginning to discuss James's childhood, his relationships with his mother and father, and what shaped him.

From the stories I heard from him and his family, he was a shy and quiet child, a respectful son, and close to his mother. His father was one of several brothers in an Italian immigrant family who had started a small grocery store that, in one generation, became a successful public company. The enormous, almost unparalleled success of that business defined the trajectory of James' life and the lives of his family. They were celebrities in our small town.

As James grew up there was an unspoken expectation that he would be part of the next generation to run the company. He used to say, "No one ever asked me what I wanted to be when I grew up; I never got to dream of being anything other than part of the business my father and uncles created."

4

His father and uncles were all distinctively brilliant as entrepreneurs and visionaries. What they built in a relatively short amount of time was extraordinary. The Bruno brothers were outgoing men who created a kind and familial environment in their stores. I'm not sure they fully understood the astonishingly unusual culture they forged with thousands of employees. It could have been a Wharton's Business School course on building a successful business culture. They were engaged with their employees, knew every employee by name, and were constantly in the stores, not hidden in the corporate office.

I've often had Bruno's employees come up to me, excited and proud, to tell me stories about how James' dad or one of his uncles went out of their way to ask about their children or to send food and help when there was a crisis in their family. It was a big business that ran like a small family company.

James did not have the temperament of the men in his family. He was not naturally outgoing. He was smart and intuitive in business but happiest when he was quiet and working alone.

Where he was like his family was in his generosity and kindness, it defined him. James was the gentlest of men. He walked softly in the world, always aware of others and willing to be of service. Anyone who knew him was drawn to his quiet, kind nature. He was thoughtful in unexpected ways, in little ways, and big ways.

After he died, one of his fraternity brothers came to see me. He spent the afternoon telling me funny and sweet stories about James in college at the University of Alabama in Tuscaloosa. One defining story of James's nature was the night he went out with friends. Tuscaloosa is a typical college town with a main street near campus cluttered with bars and restaurants. He and a

5

few guys had walked over from campus to hang out. There was a downpour just as they were trying to get back to their dorms. Rather than take care of himself, James gave his two buddies his umbrella and rain jacket, ran back in the rain, and got drenched. That was the spirit of him. He loved to care for others. And he often put himself last.

Since his death, I've often wondered about always putting himself last. He was so much fun, had a delightful, deprecating sense of humor, and his selflessness didn't seem gratuitous. But I've wondered about the undercurrent meaning of it.

When he talked about his childhood and teenage years, there was such sadness when he described how he felt he had disappointed his father and family. The depth of those feelings seemed to have magnified in the year after his father's death.

Again, we were four weeks into COVID, and the whole world seemed highly anxious and increasingly depressed. The world was shutting down around us. No one had any answers or ideas about what would become of us as a civilization.

James' anxiety and depression didn't seem strangely out of line or misplaced, given all that was happening around us. In retrospect, I now understand how closely he was guarding his pain, not allowing me to know his plans.

When I arrived that Friday evening, I asked him what was wrong. He said he hadn't been feeling well and that his stomach was upset. We sat on the sofa for a while and talked. I can't remember what. He asked me to sit close and put my head on his shoulder. I had no idea that would be the last time I would ever put my head on his shoulder.

I woke up Saturday morning at 8:00 to the phone ringing beside my bed. It was James. I hadn't heard him get up that morning. He said he was at his office doing some work. Again, he mentioned that he wasn't feeling well, and I told him we didn't have to go to the lake if he wasn't up to it. He answered, "No, let's stick to the plan." As we were hanging up, he told me he loved me; his phone clicked off as I said, "I love you too."

We talked about him picking me up around 10:00. I quickly got dressed and started packing a cooler to take to the lake. I lined up the bags of sunflower seeds to load into his car, along with my clothes for the weekend, the cooler, and some new pots and pans I had bought.

Ten o'clock rolled around, and James wasn't there yet. He was rarely late; if so, he always called or texted to let me know. I tried texting and calling him but got no answer. I started playing the piano, working on a new Chopin piece I wanted to learn, trying to pass the time. I assumed he must have stopped at the grocery store to pick up a few last-minute things. I even remember thinking that maybe there was no cell service at Publix, where he usually shopped.

After I texted him a few more times with no response, I began shaking uncontrollably, shaking from the inside out. He had told me the night before and that morning on the call that he wasn't feeling well. Had he had a heart attack? Where was he? Something was wrong for him not to be answering me.

I got in my car, knowing that he was not okay. I was shaking so badly I could hardly drive. I first drove to the Publix near us, praying that his car would be in the parking lot. His car was not there. I prayed he got tied up at the office and was running late. I started driving to his office, about fifteen minutes away.

My heart sank when I crested the hill to his office, and his car was parked in its usual spot. It was a Saturday morning, and no one else was in the office. I ran to his office door, praying that he was okay, but the door was locked. I banged and banged and banged on the door. He didn't answer.

I called 911, and within a few minutes, the police and firemen were there. They pried open the door. I screamed for him as I rounded the corner to his conference room.

He was there. Laying on the floor. He had taken his life at 8:10 that morning, seconds after he hung up the phone with me.

It never occurred to me that he would take his life. That was not something I thought was possible for us as a couple, as a family, as a mother and father. We loved our boys so much. Their welfare was always our priority. That thought truly never entered my mind.

The days and weeks that followed were a blur of pain, unanswered questions, sobbing and sorrow, anger and disbelief. I was heartbroken.

I don't know when the grieving process starts. I was a mess of so many emotions. There didn't seem to be a path out of it. But there was one thing that began to happen. I started writing to him. It might sound macabre, but I wrote him a letter every Saturday morning, telling him what I felt. I asked him every question I had about why he did it. I begged him to take care of the boys. I begged him to keep his spirit close to us.

Sometimes, I was furious with him, and most of the time, I wept uncontrollably when I wrote. The only positive turn I could make in those early days was to be grateful for all he gave us with his life.

A Prayer of Gratitude

I am so grateful for James' life. He was such a light in the world. I'm so grateful for our beautiful boys and how he helped shape them. They are both like him in so many ways. Thank you.

Chapter 2

Grief and Sorrow

I've learned so much about survival in the last five years. Tools in my grief journey that have been tremendously helpful to me. I hope what I've experienced can be a roadmap for others navigating their pain, but I'm only five years into this journey. My sister often uses this analogy about growth; she says, "I'm only at the base camp of Mt. Everest." I've struggled and wept my way to that base camp, but she's right; I'm about halfway up an arduous climb, and it has taken me five years to get here. I can see the huge, high summit above me. It's not nearly as far away as it used to be, but I haven't made the final ascent yet. I hope my story will be filled out in another five years with more tools and wisdom. But here's where I am now.

Before I can begin to share the survival tools that have become my roadmap, taking me out of shame, fear, and the pain of loss, I would be remiss not to talk about the beginning story of my grief.

The story of grief is rough. It's the bow-breaking ocean of sadness and sorrow that comes with tragedy, loss, and betrayal.

I'm often asked by others who are going through the suicide

or loss of a loved one, "How long will this pain last? When will I ever feel okay again?"

I remember asking exactly those same questions.

For me, grief has been different from all other emotions. I had to figure out how to live with it; to walk with it, to sleep with it, to eat with it, to bathe with it. Learning to continue to live with the pain of grief became the first thin blanket of healing.

It sounds strange to say that grief was healing. It wasn't the grief itself, though I believe we must weep and mourn on the deepest soul level. One of the first tiny pinpoints of light for me was understanding that the grief wasn't going anywhere for a while but that I could live; I could survive alongside the grief.

Grief is not something you overcome. It's not something you fight. It's an emotion you get to know. You learn to continue living while grieving. That's not what anyone wants to hear. I certainly didn't. I was desperate for anything that would speed up the process, that would get me out of my pain.

The hardest realization, one that took some time for me to metabolize, was that James wasn't coming back. That has been the most difficult reality of my life.

I chose to go on living even though it was awful. Some days, I didn't want to choose life. I wanted to stay in bed, pull the covers over my head, and pretend it was all a bad dream.

I had to live in two worlds. I lived in the busyness of the life I had built. I had to keep running my business. I had to take care of the house. I had to be as emotionally present as possible to help my children. That was one life. Running parallel to that was a life of grief. That life was a constant and powerful ache. It was sorrow piled upon sorrow, always present, always pressing. I toggled back and forth between those two worlds throughout my days and nights.

Julia Samuel, a grief psychotherapist, has a powerful quote that was helpful to me in understanding my early days of grief. She said, "… grief unmasks our greatest fears, strips away our layers of protection, and reveals our innermost selves."

Grief and sorrow are intensely personal. Everyone navigates their grief differently. For me, the early days of grief were defined by fear. Fear of even the smallest tasks became overwhelming.

James had handled so much of our life: our finances, managing the house, our cars, and our insurance. I was lost at first.

Fear was so odd for me. I had lived my life big, taking risks and not afraid of much. I had successes and failures along the way, but I always managed to get back up and try again. This was different.

Fear, the fear that comes from grief, makes absolutely no sense. It's not logical.

I grew up surrounded by various faith practices, but it wasn't until my early twenties that I started reading spiritual writers and thinkers to explore and shape my personal beliefs. I am still immersed in that journey today. One of the writers I was drawn to in those early years and continue to learn from is the great C.S. Lewis. Years before, I read his book, *A Grief Observed*, in which he wrote about the death of his wife, Joy, from cancer. After James died, I pulled that book from my study shelf, thinking it was likely too erudite to help me. Yet, as often happens when seeking help, something arrives exactly when we need it. I opened the book, and it fell to the page where Lewis writes, "No one ever told me that grief felt so like fear."

In that moment, understanding washed over me. I realized I was not alone in my fear; C. S. Lewis had walked this painful path before me and knew exactly what I was experiencing. His words offered me comfort and a reminder that others had felt this same devasting grief and fear.

In the first months after James died, I didn't want to see anyone or go anywhere. I didn't want the stares of those who felt sorry for me, and I didn't want the questions from those who were bold enough to ask.

It was the early days of COVID and doing anything was difficult. I remember a specific day when I needed to go to the grocery store. I was masked up, had my sanitizing wipes ready to wipe down the grocery cart, and drove to a store just minutes from our house. But I couldn't make myself go in. I sat in the parking lot and tried to talk down the fear, but I was paralyzed by it. I couldn't move. I could not open the car door and make myself walk into the store. I don't know how to qualify or define that fear other than to say I felt controlled by it. It was powerful.

Finally, I decided I would drive to a grocery store that wasn't near our home so that, hopefully, I wouldn't see anyone I knew. I drove to the opposite side of town, and again, I couldn't get out of the car. It made no sense to me. I wanted to fight and reason through it, but I couldn't.

At times, you feel in control and like you can handle things, and then the debilitating, paralyzing effects of grief storm your insides.

Nothing about my life was like it was before he died. Life with James was the antithesis of the chaos I felt after he died.

Our life together had been predictable in ways that felt like protection—predictable in that wonderful, everyday boredom of a long, trusting partnership. That predictability was something I craved.

I loved being able to count on the daily rituals with James. He always made my morning coffee, and we discussed the day ahead. I worked longer hours than he did, and he loved to cook, so dinner was often waiting, with a glass of wine being poured as he heard my car come into the garage. We went to the lake on weekends or hiked at a nearby state park. He chose the best of the new movies, screening them for what would be a good fit for us. James blanketed our lives with niceness.

Those are the little things, the ordinary things that gave shape to my days and ground beneath my feet. I felt protected by those rituals, and I felt protected by James.

His death, those early days of learning to adapt to a wholly different life without him, felt like total chaos inside me. I did not choose the change that was forced on me. The change, the differentness of my new life, the fear of all I didn't know how to do without him. It was forced on me by his death, and even though I couldn't admit it, it was forced on me by him. The person I trusted most in the world had paved the way for this sorrow, this pain, this anguish by choosing to take his life.

I asked myself all the usual questions when someone we love takes his life. How could I have helped keep him here? Why didn't I see what he was planning to do? Why, why, why?

My youngest son had just graduated from college when James died. He and James had such a sweet, close relationship. They were in constant contact, talking almost daily and always in touch via text.

When I had to tell him what had happened to his dad, he sank to the floor in sobs and said, "Mama, if he loved me so much, why wasn't I enough to keep him here?"

I've since learned that shame, guilt, and the endless questions of *why* after experiencing the loss of a loved one to suicide are universal among survivors.

Death of a partner, a spouse, a child, a friend, or a sibling is, by any definition, a harsh truth that we are ill-equipped to deal with. Death is a topic we are silent about in our culture. We don't have the words to voice how frightening it is and how much we want to shield it from happening to us. But suicide has ever so much more stigma and discomfort around it.

The irony is that no matter how broken you are or how intense the grief and sorrow are, life goes on. It doesn't stop because you are grieving and fighting for your life.

Several weeks after James died, there was a night when an enormous storm was headed in our direction. Tornados are a regular occurrence in Birmingham, and we were bracing for a long, rough night. Our family room had floor-to-ceiling windows all along the back of the house— the direction of the storm's onslaught. At the height of the storm, while lightning and thunder were raging and the wind was shaking the house, the huge windows that made up the entire family room wall began to slip down in their frames. As the glass descended several inches, rain poured into the house. Not small amounts of rain, but more rain than all the towels in the house could mop up. And then, the bugs started coming in. I don't mean mosquitoes and ants. The giant palmetto bugs that live in the trees in the South were coming into my house by the dozen! I'm terrified of roaches. I can handle almost any other bug or rodent, but those things terrify me.

At first, I frantically tried to manage the rain coming into the house. I was crying, running around with towels and buckets, and so mad at James for leaving me with such a mess. How could he have left me with windows falling out of their frames?

It was a moment when I wanted to give up. It also underscored the stark reality that I was on my own. I had no choice but to figure it out. James was not coming back.

When it dawned on me that no number of towels, pots, or buckets could remedy the situation, I sat on the floor and cried, and then I laughed hysterically. There I was in my pajamas, sitting in a flood with flying "locusts"—the biblical metaphor did not escape me.

All the literature you read about grief tells you to stay close to family and friends and to try to share your feelings about your loss. In the first months after James died, everything I read about grief and surviving just made me mad. I did not want to talk about my life and what happened. I did not want to talk about James. I was angry. Deeply angry.

I didn't think anyone could possibly understand what I was feeling. Nor did I trust anyone not to judge me or blame me. I went into a place of complete isolation.

My situation was exacerbated by the fact that James died one month into COVID. I was isolating because of my grief because I could not face the world without James in it. However, the whole world was isolating. There was an enormous collective fear surrounding this global virus and the unknown facing our world. At any other time, there would have been people reaching out to me, visiting me, trying to help me survive. The truth was that everyone was trying to isolate and survive.

The big Italian family James came from was well-known and respected in the business community. If it weren't for COVID, his funeral would have been packed with friends, fraternity brothers, colleagues, and his beloved church community. But that was not at all what his funeral was. Because of COVID and the early rules about congregating, we were only allowed ten people in the church for his funeral, including the priests.

Looking back, I don't know if it was helpful or horrible not to have friends and family at his funeral. My boys were on either side of me with their respective girlfriends on either side of them. James' three sisters sat scattered around the small chapel to obey the rules of 'distancing.' A niece and nephew snuck in, and two priests officiated. Twelve people to mourn a life silenced entirely too early. Twelve people to celebrate the kindest man we had ever known.

After the service, we returned to our house, just the five of us— which felt strange. I'm sure we all longed for the love and nurturing from friends and family in the ways we are used to, with a community surrounding us in death. At the time, one of my clients was a regional fast-food chain. The CEO was a good and faithful friend throughout those days after James' death. He knew my boys loved Jack's chicken and had sent enough fried chicken, mashed potatoes, biscuits, and coleslaw to feed about thirty people. It was comfort food at its finest and a huge amount of food for our small group. It made us all laugh. A welcome relief.

A Prayer of Gratitude

Thank you that one day, the work of grief will be done. Thank you that sorrow knows its way within me and will find its way out. Thank you that there will be a time when the wounds of this loss will heal.

Chapter 3

Prayers and Miracles

A guardian angel painting hung over my bed when I was a little girl. She was bathed in golden-pink light; to my child's eyes, she was the epitome of beauty. I would stare at her, captivated, whispering my prayers. In my childlike faith, I believed she could calm the angry voices in the hallway, soften the slamming doors, and bring peace to the confusion around me. Her presence offered a sense of protection, a small pocket of safety in a home that often felt unsafe.

At night, I would pray to her soft glow, imagining her wings stretching over me, her light a shield against the world's unpredictability. In those moments, I felt an invisible hand steady my racing heart.

My prayers were simple—pleas for safety, for comfort, for something better than the storm of my reality. It wasn't just a prayer to a painted image but to something bigger, a sense of God I couldn't yet articulate.

My earliest understanding of God was this innate consciousness of something greater—a love that felt different from the turmoil I knew.

When I was eight, our family unraveled under the weight of illness and abandonment, I felt this presence as a protective force, guiding me away from danger and holding me up when I had no one to lean on.

My family and extended family had an underpinning of faith and Christian tradition. My grandmother and her sisters were daughters of a Methodist minister, and their voices were always lifted in prayer and hymns. My parents professed belief in God, but the dissonance between their faith and the anger and betrayal that filled our home left me confused.

If God was good, if He truly cared, why was my world so broken?

Even as a child, I kept my faith separate from religion—the religion of my parents, grandmother, and aunts. I couldn't reconcile the image of a good God with the harsh reality of my life at home. Instead, I turned inward, seeking the God I felt, who seemed to meet me in my deepest fears and moments of doubt.

Prayer, though, always came easily to me. As a little girl, I prayed constantly and often walked the quiet streets of my small town, spilling out my heart as I walked.

"Help me," I would whisper. "Show me a way out."

My dear friend and pastor Tracy Clark, says, "Your connection to God is your most sacred connection. It is the one that will lead you back to the healing of your spirit. It is the one that will allow you to open your intuition and break free of fear."

Looking back, I see how those childhood prayers were answered subtly yet profoundly. There weren't grand gestures that changed everything at once but steady opportunities and happenings that illuminated my path, creating an invisible thread that seemed to weave moments of goodness into my life.

The first—and perhaps the most transformative—was the gift of music. It entered my life like a lifeline, wrapping around me in a way nothing else could. Music was my refuge and marked my doorway to something greater.

It was certainly an escape, but it was like walking through a door into a world of beauty, structure, and meaning. Through music, I found myself surrounded by incredible teachers who didn't just nurture my talent but, more importantly, nurtured my spirit. They saw something I couldn't yet see in myself and held that vision steady when my world felt anything but constant. Each note I played, each piece I learned, felt like it tethered me to a sense of purpose and belonging.

Music became a place where I could feel God's presence without needing to define God or have answers. It was in the rise and fall of melodies, the discipline of practice, and the sheer beauty of sound that I began to sense the divine. It grounded me when I felt unsteady and allowed me to express what I couldn't say aloud.

For nearly two decades, music carried me, offering light where I saw none and teaching me an early sense of resilience and hope.

There were other miracles, too, smaller but no less significant. One moment stands out like a flash of lightning in my memory—a moment that, in hindsight, feels like divine intervention.

I was nine years old, walking the quiet streets of our little town alone; a sense of independence mingled with the vulnerability of my youth. Out of nowhere, a car slowed to a crawl beside me. The window rolled down, and a stranger leaned out, his voice soft yet insistent. He tried to coax me closer, offering me candy and to see the puppy in the backseat. My petite frame froze for a moment as I processed the situation. But then, like a sudden, undeniable force, a deep, urgent knowing gripped me—a surge of something much larger than instinct. RUN.

Without thinking, I screamed and bolted, my feet pounding against the pavement, my heart racing as fast as my legs could carry me. I didn't look back until I was safely home, trembling and breathless. The terror lingered, but so did the sense that I had been protected by something unseen, something sacred. At nine years old, I didn't have the words to name it, but now, I would call it a miracle. It wasn't just luck or quick thinking—it was a divine whisper, a nudge from God, sparing me from dangers I didn't fully understand then but shudder to imagine now.

Looking back, that moment became one of many that confirmed my belief in a loving God who watches over us, even in our smallest, most vulnerable moments. It wasn't just about escaping danger; it was about the presence of something larger than myself that felt deeply personal and protective. It was as if the universe itself had stepped in, reminding me that I was seen, that I was cared for.

And it wasn't the only time. Moments like these happened throughout my childhood, each a miracle of protection that left an imprint on my soul.

The divine didn't always appear with blinding light or parting seas; sometimes, it came in the form of an internal nudge, a surge of clarity, or a forceful urge to move, to scream, or to run. These miracles were as real to me as the ground beneath my feet, shaping not only my belief in God but also my understanding of how deeply interwoven faith and survival can be.

And then there was my aunt Darlene. She was just four years older than me, more like a sister than an aunt. With her, I felt a kind of safety I couldn't find at home. She was my refuge, a light in a world that often felt too heavy for a child to carry. Darlene and I created a little universe of joy and trust, one where the turmoil of the adult world couldn't reach us.

We'd jump rope in the yard, giggling until we fell over, breathless from laughter. Sometimes, we'd play hide-and-seek in the bushes. Whispering secrets and dreams as though the trees and leaves were our best friends. With her, I felt cherished, like I truly belonged.

Darlene radiated joy and a sense of fun that gave me courage. She had a way of making me believe that magic and innocence still existed. Her laughter was infectious, and her sweetness helped heal my wounded heart.

In her presence, I began to understand what it felt like to be seen and loved for who I was. In her beautiful child's way, she pulled me closer to a sense of God and love without ever needing to say it out loud. She lived it with me.

Like music, Darlene was a miracle in my life. She reminded me that even in the darkest times, there could be pockets of light and joy. She gave me a sense of strength and bravery, encouraging me to keep going and believe in a better world.

Her companionship taught me that love, even in its simplest form, has the profound power to heal. To this day, she remains one of my most trusted friends and allies. Through every milestone and challenge, she has championed, advocated for, and cheered me on in everything I've done. When James died, she was there, walking alongside me every step of the way. Her unwavering presence is one of the greatest gifts of my life.

These early miracles—music, protection, and the love of people like Darlene—shaped me in ways I can only now fully understand. They nurtured a soft, intuitive part of me that could still sense goodness and believe in a God who loved me.

Looking back, I see that my life was always held by something greater, a divine presence that whispered, "Keep going. You are not alone."

These miracles, both big and small, wrapped a safety net around my childhood, catching me before I fell too far. They were murmurs of God's love, guiding me toward a life that, despite its hardships, was rich with meaning and purpose.

As my life unfolded, my belief in God and the miracles that touched my daily existence became my cornerstone, the thread that wove everything together. From my earliest encounter with the Guardian angel over my bed, my understanding of God was personal and intimate—a relationship shaped not by doctrine or dogma but by an unshakable sense of presence and connection.

Organized religion felt rigid to me, confining what I believed was an infinite and loving energy. But prayer—that was where I found my truth.

When I married and became a mother, prayer became even more essential. Suddenly, my life was no longer just about me. It was about these people I loved so deeply—people whose needs and dreams often outweighed my own. I needed wisdom beyond myself to navigate the challenges and joys of family life, so I leaned into prayer with intensity.

I pleaded with God to let me keep the baby that was growing inside me but was not thriving. And I jumped up and down with thanksgiving for the birth of that first healthy baby. I whispered prayers in the quiet moments of nursing a child and in the chaos of school mornings.

In the quiet of the night, after bedtime stories and the last snuggles, I was often struck by the profound contrast between my life and the one I had come from. There were moments when I would sit in the stillness, marveling at the beauty of my family—the love that surrounded me, the stability of a marriage built on partnership, and the incredible blessing of healthy, joyful children. It felt like I was living the biggest miracle—one that God had been quietly weaving into the fabric of my life all along.

That awareness often left me gobsmacked. The pain and instability of my childhood hadn't defined me; instead, it had been transformed into the very foundation of the life I was now privileged to build.

I realized that miracles weren't confined to dramatic, once-in-a-lifetime events. They were in the everyday—the laughter of my children, the quiet strength of my marriage, the sense of purpose and joy that had replaced the uncertainty I once knew. They were the small and steady blessings that, over time, had created a life so full of goodness that I could hardly believe it was my own.

Just like when I was a child, prayer was easy and constant, not because it solved every problem but because it reminded me that I wasn't walking alone. My connection to God was a living, breathing relationship that evolved and deepened as I grew. While I resisted labels and rigid beliefs, my faith remained steady. There was always that still, small voice that said, "You are loved. You are guided. Keep going."

And then, the unthinkable happened—my husband of twenty-nine years took his life. That moment shattered the world I had so carefully built. Where was God then? Where was the God I had prayed to and trusted so deeply? Where was He when everything I believed about my marriage and the life we created together unraveled in an instant?

And yet, somehow in the aftermath of James' death, my belief in God remained unbroken. It is strange to think about now—how I could hold onto that faith even as I wrestled with anger, confusion, and heartbreak. Nothing made sense—my carefully constructed belief system collided with the reality of loss in a way that felt cruelly contradictory.

I shouted my questions into the void, demanded answers, and let my anger spill over into prayers that were more like cries of desperation. How could a loving God allow this to happen? How could the safety of my world be obliterated in an instant? I felt betrayed, unmoored, and shattered.

While everything else crumbled—the foundation of my marriage, the safety of my home, the trust I had in the life we'd built—my faith remained. It wasn't the tidy faith of childhood or the confident faith of young adulthood. It was bruised and battered.

Once again, my prayers became my lifeline. They were no longer the quiet, hopeful whispers of a woman navigating daily life. They were desperate cries from the depths of despair, raw and unfiltered, pleading for something—anything—that could help me hang on. My prayers were for survival, for a thread of hope to believe in life again.

It felt impossible to reconcile my unwavering faith in God with the loss I was enduring. How could the God I trusted allow this? But even in the storm, I clung to Him—not with answers but with the tiniest shred of belief that He was still there. I prayed not for understanding but for endurance. I prayed for strength to keep breathing, to wake up each morning, and to move through the unbearable.

Prayer became the raw, guttural act of reaching out for a presence I couldn't see but could still feel, faintly, somewhere in the shadows of my grief. Perhaps it is strange—or even miraculous—that my belief in a good God did not waver.

Grief and prayer became my constant companions in those first days. They stitched me together in ways I didn't understand or realize. I didn't have a sudden healing or revelation—I was on a slow, stumbling journey toward believing that even in my darkest hour, life could still hold a trace of the divine.

Prayer of Gratitude

Thank you, God, for the unwavering presence of your love and guidance. For the whispers that have led me through darkness and for the miracles, both large and small, that have carried me through life's most challenging moments. Thank you for the strength to hold on to prayer.

Chapter 4

A Defiant Gratitude

Before this grief journey, if I had read my own words, defining gratitude as an act of defiance, I would likely have scoffed at the writer and presumed that she didn't understand the meaning of gratitude. As strange as it may sound, being grateful for the ordinary and the extraordinary in the early days after James's death became a stalwart stance—my way of saying, "Grief will not kill me."

When I thought about how gratitude looked for me in those early days, I remembered how it emerged from an unexpected place within. Gratitude in the first part of my survival journey was not one of gentle gratefulness but one of stalwart defiance.

Here's my story of a defiant gratitude in the midst of grief.

That spring, after James died, I spent countless mornings sitting by the window in our den, watching the world come to life outside. The trees blossomed, the birds sang, and the days lengthened, but I felt frozen in place, unsure how to follow the rhythm of renewal unfolding around me. James was gone, and with him, my will—my will to live and my purpose for living.

29

My grief was vast and consuming. It was a constant weight that felt like I was continuously looking through a gray lens. The color had been dialed out of my world.

One morning, as I stared out that same window, I could see the herb garden James planted for me just a month before he died. It was a little overgrown in parts but mainly thriving. Seeing it stirred something in me, melting my numbness for a moment. It was a fragile gratitude, mirroring how I felt on the inside. At that moment, the memory of his love and thoughtfulness brought a little light to the darkness inside me. That tremor of a feeling of thankfulness marked the beginning of an unexpected journey of gratitude.

In today's world, "gratitude" can feel hollow and overworked, a buzzword pasted onto social media posts alongside artfully staged photos of sunsets or steaming mugs of coffee. It's marketed as a quick fix—list three things, and your life will transform. All gratitude is beneficial and shifts us toward a focus on the positive. I'm certainly not discounting that; however, the gratitude I found in grief was not remotely like that. It wasn't easy or polished. It wasn't about ignoring pain or pasting on a smile. It was raw, messy, and hard-won.

Each moment of gratitude was pulled from the depths of my sorrow, and I clung to it with fierce determination. It forced me to confront the broken pieces of my world and find meaning in the chaos. Gratitude, in this form, was not a quiet reflection—it was a fierce act of rebellion against the consuming grief.

It was my first step of walking forward, out of abject grief and sorrow, ultimately toward a path of survival. I didn't consciously know that then. At that point survival seemed like a fragmented dream, far out of my reach.

In the five years since James's passing, I've had the humbling privilege of walking beside others through their valleys and grief. Each story is unique, yet one thread binds them all together: how people harness their pain.

For some, anger becomes their fuel—a fierce, consuming fire that drives them toward healing. They channel their rage into action, charging a path forward through the sheer force of their will. I've witnessed this and admired its power, but my journey took shape differently.

In the immediate aftermath of James's death, gratitude was the furthest thing from my mind. My world had shattered into a million pieces, and I had no idea where even to begin picking them up. I stumbled through a haze of confusion and sorrow, barely finding the strength to get out of bed each morning.

It's not something many people want to admit, and few are willing to talk about it, but surviving the suicide of a spouse feels like a profound betrayal—of everything you trusted, everything you built your family on, everything you believed love to be. It tears apart the foundation of how you understand life and leaves you questioning everything. There were days when I didn't think I could go on.

I could put on a brave face for my boys, show up for work, and care for my employees, but the truth is, the nights were unbearable. The isolation of grief felt insurmountable, like darkness I couldn't escape.

Early on, I was desperate for something—anything—to hold onto just to make it through the day, especially for my children. Gratitude didn't appear as an intentional practice. Instead, it emerged as a flicker of my will, a will I had always carried deep within me. Before, it had driven me to succeed, to explore, to live boldly. But after James, that will was almost extinguished.

In my darkest moments, my will was entirely tied to my boys. More than anything, I wanted to show them that we could survive. That we could rebuild. That we would find a way to be a family again, even when I doubted my own ability to lead us there.

Gratitude became a small lifeline, though not in the way one might expect. At first, it wasn't a heartfelt, intentional feeling— it was a distraction, a way to momentarily lift myself from the crushing weight of grief. It seemed paradoxical to the very idea of gratitude, but it gave me just enough energy to keep going.

It felt like I was in a boxing ring. Grief would hit me so hard I'd collapse, unable to rise. I'd roll over, tempted to give up completely, but then, that determination to survive—for my boys, for myself —would force me back to my feet. Gratitude became the spark that lit that determination, even when I felt hollow inside.

It wasn't soft or gentle—it was defiant, a refusal to be swallowed by grief. In the depths of my sorrow, gratitude became a form of resistance. Each moment I chose to see the good or the beautiful felt like a victory. I clung to it with stubborn determination, knowing that this act was a way of saying, "I'm still here. Grief can't kill me."

When James passed away, people often said, "Focus on the good times" or "Be thankful for the years you had together." Their words were meant to comfort me, but instead, they made me furious. Gratitude felt impossible. It wasn't something I could summon with platitudes or force myself to feel.

In those early days, gratitude also felt like an insult to my grief. I wasn't ready to 'move on' or 'look on the bright side.' What I eventually came to understand, however, was that gratitude wasn't about dismissing my pain or pretending it didn't exist.

Robert Emmons, a leading researcher on gratitude, describes it as the ability to affirm the good in life even while facing hardship. Gratitude doesn't minimize pain; it places it in context. It lets us say, *Yes, this hurts—but there's still beauty here.*

For me, that realization came in small, fleeting moments. Each morning, I challenged myself to notice things I was grateful for, even though many mornings, being thankful for anything was the opposite of how I felt.

I learned to be thankful for a bird landing on the windowsill and the roses that bloomed outside the bedroom window just after his death. These were not extraordinary things, but they shifted my focus away from my sorrow, even if only for a few minutes.

One morning, as I sat with my notebook open, I wrote the words, *I loved how James laughed.* The moment the words spilled onto the page it was as if a dam inside me burst. For weeks, I had been holding my memories of James at a careful distance, afraid that allowing them too close would undo me completely. But this was different. The words released a torrent of sorrow and, at the same time, drenched me in unexpected gratitude—for how his laughter could light up a room and for the thoughtful tenderness he infused into our family. I was still mad at him and hadn't resolved that yet, but I was allowing myself to feel again. To feel all the goodness of James and what we had built as a family. It sounds like a crazy mixed-up ball of disparate emotions, and it was. But it was also honest. An honesty I needed to hold what was so good and amazing and beautiful about James and also honor the gut-wrenching path I was on to survive his death.

For the first time, I realized that gratitude wasn't a betrayal of my grief. That moment marked a pivotal shift. Gratitude became the foundation I leaned on not to forget James or move on without him but to carry him forward with me, woven into my everyday life. It's impossible to live twenty-nine years with someone and turn off all that those years meant because your spouse chose not to continue living.

Gratitude wasn't an antidote to the pain but a companion to it, as I learned to navigate a world without him.

In the months that followed, gratitude became a trusted survival tool. Whenever my therapist asked how I was coping with the hard realities of life without James, I would answer, "I'm trying to turn it into gratitude." I think, at first, she believed I was in denial, using it to avoid facing the depths of my pain. But the truth was, I had discovered that even the smallest grain of gratitude—a fleeting memory, the scent of the roses, thoughts of my boys—could reframe my sorrow.

I realized that grief and gratitude weren't adversaries but two forces working together in a delicate, transformative dance. They weren't about canceling each other out but about learning to carry both at once—grief in one hand, gratitude in the other. I learned to balance them determinedly as I weaved threads of gratitude into my sorrow.

I didn't understand then that this practice marked the beginning of a deeper spiritual journey. Gratitude, born out of intense pain and struggle became a force that informed my spirit and reshaped how I moved through the world.

I didn't yet have the language for it—words like energy movement, vibration, and frequency— but it was as though I was already living those spiritual concepts. Each time I practiced gratitude, even in my darkest moments, I could feel something change within. The weight of sorrow lifted, if only a little, and a glimmer of hope appeared.

Every time I chose gratitude, I shifted my energy. I invited a higher power—God and The Universe—to open the door for light and Divine intervention.

As gratitude began to carve small openings of light into my grief, I noticed another shift emerging. Grief, in its rawest form, turns our gaze inward, narrowing our world until all we see is our own pain. It consumes us, leaving little room for anything else.

That's the nature of loss: it's profoundly isolating. But gratitude—particularly the kind born out of suffering—possesses a quiet power to widen that narrow focus. It gently lifts us from our inward focus and opens the door to empathy.

As overwhelming as my loss was, I began to have a new awareness of the pain and suffering of others around me. Their struggles might not have mirrored mine, but they were there—raw, painful, and heavy, just like mine.

I remember a friend coming to visit me, in theory, to console me, but when she sat down, she began to pour out the details of her divorce. Her heartbreak was palpable and spilled into my already overflowing cup of grief. It could have felt insensitive in the middle of my overwhelming sorrow; however, my heart understood her pain in a way I never could have before losing James.

Those encounters began repeating themselves as though I were a magnet for others suffering. I quickly realized people weren't turning to me for answers or solutions. They needed someone who could sit with them in their grief and wouldn't flinch or turn away.

Losing James in such a tragic, unimaginable way had cracked

me wide open emotionally. I believe that opening allows others to feel seen in their pain.

I don't think people realized what drew them to me, but they could see that I was living through sorrow and turned to me as a companion in suffering.

I fought with all my being to survive, find meaning, and figure out how to live again. Somehow, during that fight, I was gifted with the strength to bear witness to the pain and suffering of others.

Once you've been through immense sorrow and suffering, your empathy seems to come forward without judgment or comparison. I was constantly reminded that while our tragedies may differ, the human experience of loss is universal.

Gratitude born from pain and struggle was guiding me toward a new purpose. I didn't know what it was yet, but I felt pulled to something that would make sense of my own suffering while connecting me to the suffering of others.

Prayer of Gratitude

Thank you for the determined will of the human spirit—to survive despite our sorrow and suffering. Thank you for the beauty of human connection— to share our pain and help each other heal. Thank you for the ever-present invitation to life, to go forward, and to live.

Chapter 5

Get Your Feet on the Ground, Theresa!

I t's late on a Saturday afternoon, and I'm sitting in my office watching an enormous thunderstorm roll in. Its prolific display of power is both fascinating and frightening. In South Florida, we experience almost daily thunderstorms, replete with magnificent light shows. It's mesmerizing to watch. My little dog, Jules, is at my feet. He's undoubtedly more frightened than fascinated.

I've been drawn to the small wonders and grand displays of nature's miracles from as early as I can remember. A flower, a butterfly, a beautiful leaf, or the stars always captured me as a child, pulling me into a place I didn't fully understand then. I couldn't name it, but I knew it was sacred. The beauty of nature drew me into what, in my child's heart, I thought God might be. It gave me a deep sense of protection and comfort.

After James died, nature became an unexpected source of healing. In those early days of grief, I couldn't stop the tears; they flowed without end. I was drowning in them, unable to find anything that could bring relief. One day, a spiritual teacher told me, "Theresa, you've got to get outside. Put your feet on the earth."

I understood her words but assumed she was suggesting I distract myself by going outside for a walk.

Walking and hiking in beautiful places has always been a refuge for me—one of my favorite things to do. Wherever I was in the world, the first thing I sought out was a place to walk and hike, to reconnect to nature and Spirit.

After James passed, the idea of returning to the outdoors felt utterly different. It was one more thing I had to face without him, one more thing that had been central to our life together.

James and I often hiked at a state park about 20 minutes from our home. It had lots of gorgeous trails deep in the woods, and streams ran alongside many of them. On a weekday afternoon, it was intensely quiet, inviting the mind to open up and release stress and the demands of work.

The month before James died, the middle of March 2020, the start of the pandemic, we hiked there every afternoon. With my business shifting to Zoom and long hours in front of the computer, we agreed I would wrap up my days by 4 p.m. so we could escape into nature and stillness. James always had water and snacks ready for us, and those hours on the trails became a wonderful respite. The park was quiet, nearly empty, except for a few masked fellow hikers, and the spring air was alive with blooming trees and flowers. It felt like freedom after the long, suffocating days indoors, filled with Zoom meetings and the constant barrage of pandemic news.

I distinctly remember walking behind James that month, watching how he moved, listening to his voice as we talked about our days, our boys, and plans for Easter. I can still see him clearly—the way he walked, the clothes he wore, the rhythm of his presence. In those moments, the world felt grounded and normal despite everything happening around us.

After James died, I didn't have the courage to go back to that park and take those hikes. I knew I would be flooded with memories I couldn't handle, and I was afraid to hike through the woods and mountains alone. I lost James, my husband, my best friend, and strangely, I lost the healing power of those long, walks through deep, old forests with streams running alongside.

When my teacher said that I needed to get my feet on the ground and get outside, I wasn't quite sure where I could go which wasn't laden with memories of my life with James. We had spent so much of our life together exploring all the walks around our home, the state parks, and the beaches a few hours away. James knew my love for all things nature, and he integrally knew that whatever was happening in my life, being outside in beautiful woods, mountains, or near the ocean, would help center and de-stress me.

He also adored being outside, hiking up steep inclines, and seeing the views at the top. It was a fun challenge for him, and he always beat me to the top. He would wait, overlooking some incredible gorge or distant view, while I huffed and puffed my way up to meet him.

He constantly planned little getaways for us, hoping to help me take a break from my arduous work schedule and to give himself a chance to do something he loved.

I didn't feel strong enough to go to any of the places that had been 'our' places. It was just too sad and overwhelming for me to face. It took a while and some experimentation, but I finally found a safe trail with a lovely stream running beside it that I had never been to with him. And it was only ten minutes from our house. For several months, I walked on the trail day after day. I cried a lot, but every time I left the trail, tear-stained and exhausted, I felt like I had left a piece of my pain there.

I started a practice of intentionally releasing my pain, verbally and physically, to the streams and the trees. It might sound absurd, but regardless of how it sounds, there was so much healing in that simple practice. I would stand in the stream with tears running down my face; I would hold my hands out for the water and the trees to take my pain and let it wash downstream and into the earth.

It was a baptism of sorts. Not so much of being washed clean as much as having all the natural beauty around me release my sorrow.

I have always honored nature's beauty and its conduit to spiritual connectivity. I have felt closest to God in the beauty of nature, but I never realized that nature can help bear our pain.

I began to feel the arms of nature wrap around me. In nature, there is space to feel everything—our grief, anger, and longing—without needing to explain or justify it. The trees, the wind, and the stars don't ask us to be anything other than who we are in that moment. They offer us their presence, quiet wisdom, and unwavering reminder that we are never alone in our pain.

For several years, every time the pain felt like more than I could handle, I would drive as fast as I could to that trail and run to the stream. I likely looked like a mad woman to anyone who saw me, arms flailing, and tears barely held back, but it didn't matter. I was running into a sacred place of healing for my body and soul.

In all its vastness and simplicity, nature holds a timeless power to heal our souls. There is something ancient and sacred about how a tree stretches its roots deep into the earth or how a river carves its path through land.

When we find ourselves in pain—whether from loss,

betrayal, heartache— the burdens of life—it is nature that so often calls us back to ourselves. Nature reminds us that we are part of something greater that moves with us, embraces us, and holds us when we feel we cannot carry our pain. There is no judgment in nature—no expectation to be anything other than what we are. It accepts us, broken pieces and all.

The more time I spent outside, the more I began to understand what nature teaches us. I was so frustrated that it was taking me so long to walk out of my grief. I was doing as much as I knew to do— going to therapy, seeking out spiritual teachers, sitting in stillness, meditating, and praying, but sometimes, it felt like I wasn't moving forward at all.

As summer turned to fall, that first fall without James, I tentatively returned to one of the hikes we used to take. It was so hard but also immensely cleansing. I stopped at every rock outcropping where I remembered a particular conversation we'd had. I sat on a massive rock in the middle of the stream where he had sat the week before he died. I cried buckets, and I also released months of built-up fear and pain. Nature was teaching me that healing happens in its own time, naturally, just as the changing of the seasons.

I couldn't speed up my walk out of grief and pain. No one can. Everyone wants to know when the pain will end and how long grief will last. There are no answers to those questions. It is different for everyone.

Sometimes, walking barefoot in the grass or feeling the sun on our faces can bring us back from the edges of our grief. I found a silent companion in my grief journey that I desperately needed. There were days when I felt like if I was outside, in nature, I could lay my burdens down, even if just for a little while.

One of my favorite poets has always been the esteemed Mary Oliver. Her work often explored the power of nature to heal and transform us. She wrote about a deep connection with the natural world, portraying it as a source of solace, wisdom, and spiritual renewal. Oliver believed that nature could provide a refuge from the noise and the "noise of life."

For her, nature was not just a backdrop for human emotions but a companion that could guide us through grief, loneliness, and confusion. In her famous poem "Wild Geese," she urges us to be kind to ourselves. She suggests that you don't have to strive for perfection or redemption; instead, you should embrace who you are. She encourages the reader to find a place in the world and reconnect with nature and humanity.

I had long loved that poem, but it came to have a whole new meaning for me after James died. Without him, I couldn't figure out my place 'in the family of things.'

Just like friends have been essential in helping me navigate out of shame and embrace the power of self-compassion, nature became a significant force in my healing journey. When everything I thought I could rely on slipped away, and nothing felt stable, nature remained constant. It became one of my anchors.

Watching the sun rise and set each day and seeing the seasons change—these quiet, unshakable rhythms steadied me. Nature's rituals became a source of peace and grounding for me in the chaos of grief.

For years, Pema Chodron's *When Things Fall Apart* has sat on my nightstand. It's intensely beautiful and dense. I could only take it in small doses, but I kept returning to it in the months after James died. I was drawn to her writing about accepting the present moment without resistance.

Honestly, most days, I was doing the exact opposite. I was resisting everything that had happened, avoiding the present because being in it felt unbearable. I wanted to escape, to be anywhere but here, living in the pain of my reality.

But something about Chodron's words about nature resonated with me. She writes about how, in nature, we're confronted with the truth that things unfold in their own time, in their own way, and often beyond our control. Watching how eff ortlessly nature accepts all conditions—storms, droughts, the changing seasons- helped me realize I could also learn to accept my pain. That acceptance was a big step toward healing. It allowed me to stop fi ghting my suff ering and start moving through it.

Slowly, I began to see my time in the woods and on hikes as a sanctuary and a teacher. Nature was bringing me into a softer place in my suff ering, though it wasn't easy. Begrudgingly, I was learning to accept what had happened to James, to me, and to our family. It didn't come all at once; healing wasn't an avalanche.

It came in small, almost imperceptible steps. But with each one, I realized that acceptance was crucial in my healing.

Prayer of Gratitude

I'm so grateful for trees, woods, streams, and flowers.
I'm deeply grateful for the unexpected miracle of the healing
power of nature.

Chapter 6

For the Love of Jewelry

Anyone would expect that I would be in great grief and sorrow after James' death, but it was compounded by something else that kept me isolated and in hiding; that kept me from reaching out to friends. It took me a while to identify where I was staying stuck.

It was shame.

The two inflection points in my life that resulted in deep shame were James' suicide and the failure of my jewelry business. The loss of the business was minuscule compared to losing James, but that first loss had started an insidious, fast-growing virus of shame within. I lived in a relatively small Southern town ruled by old-school values. Fraud, a business closing, a suicide— I felt like I was front-page news for months.

The jewelry business was one of the things that happened in my life that sounds more like a movie than real life. I always loved jewelry. I collected it, lusted after it, studied great jewelry designers, and followed trends. But the thought of designing jewelry had never occurred to me.

As I've said before, I'm creative. I love creating almost

anything but am trained only as a pianist and filmmaker for commercial work. I had no experience designing jewelry.

For several years I spent a lot of time in Los Angeles filming commercials for my marketing business. In my free time, I began to hang out in the jewelry district in downtown LA. As I perused the stalls of people selling pearls, diamonds, and gold, I wondered if I could create pieces for myself. Again, I was not on a mission to start a business or design pieces to sell. I wanted to create pieces I envisioned that I couldn't find in the stores where I shopped.

It took a while, probably a year, of stringing bits of pearls and stones together before I had anything tangible to show.

James came to LA to visit me and the boys during the summer while I was on an extended film shoot. He loved to tell the story of walking into the house we were renting and finding me sitting cross-legged on the sofa with a huge fishing tackle box, trying to string and tie pearls. He thought it was hilarious!

After two years of more failed designs than decent ones, I found a wonderful, patient craftsman who could cast my crude drawings into gold and silver creations. At that point, I had approximately thirty pieces I had designed. I was so proud of those pieces! It had taken me two years, a lot of bravery, and downloading all the knowledge I could get my hands on to midwife those pieces into existence.

I went back to Birmingham, Alabama for the fall, getting the boys in school and getting back to daily life in my marketing firm. I had a good friend, Karen, who worked at a jewelry store where James bought most of my gifts. One night, we met for drinks, and I showed her my thirty prized possessions—strands of large, peach-colored baroque pearls tied with big chunks of paved diamond pieces. They were both edgy and feminine.

Karen had been in sales in the jewelry business for a long time. She had a keen eye for talent and had helped several young designers become successful. She looked at my pieces and said, "I think you should take these to a friend of mine in New York who owns a firm representing some of the best designers in the jewelry space."

At first, I thought it was funny—almost like a dare. And I thought she was doing the typical thing we do as Southerners; she was 'just being nice.' However, Karen forced my hand by asking if I would go to New York to meet with this firm if she could get an appointment for me. She did, and I did.

Janet Goldman, president of Fragments, is a tastemaker in the jewelry business. She has launched many great designers who have become well-known names in the industry.

The Fragments' space was impressive, with gorgeous floor-to-ceiling cases of some of the most beautiful jewelry designs I had ever seen. I felt small and deeply inadequate while I waited for Janet to look at my pieces. I was in over my head and out of my league, and I knew it.

She was tall and lithe, with long, flowing red hair. Her lack of words intimidated me. She walked over to the table where I had laid out my designs without saying anything. One by one, she picked up the pieces, examining them, turning them over in her hands, and finally said, "Darling, you have a made hand." I understood, but I had never heard that phrase before. Then, she asked if I could get her fifty more pieces in a month.

I left that meeting completely flustered. I wasn't even an incorporated business. I had no idea how to manage inventory and production and had no staff.

What in the world had I just gotten myself into?

A few weeks later, Janet partnered me with a young PR

assistant hungry for success. One of the first meetings she arranged for me was at the *New York Times*. I was naïve about how the PR business worked. I didn't have a jewelry vocabulary, background, or story other than I loved jewelry and had been inspired by my grandmother.

I left that meeting, went home to Birmingham, and put it on the back burner. I didn't rush to incorporate; I was still unsure what I wanted to do about designing jewelry as a business and Janet's request for fifty pieces.

Several weeks later, James and I were having coffee on a Sunday morning, and the phone rang. I answered to hear Karen almost screaming, "Have you seen the front page of the *New York Times Sunday Style* section?" James and I jumped up and ran to the car to get a *New York Times* Sunday paper. And there it was—a quarter page on the front of the Style Section titled "Not your Grandmother's Jewelry."

That article set in motion an otherworldly domino effect.

By the middle of the following week, Michelle Obama's stylist contacted me to ask if Mrs. Obama could wear the jewelry featured in *The Times* article to a state visit in Chile.

When Michelle Obama wore my pieces to the events in Chile, the fashion bloggers wrote about what she wore and described the jewelry in detail, several asking who had designed the pieces—I loved that I had created a bit of mystery. Within days of that press, I had dozens of stores wanting to carry the line, which was comical because there was no jewelry line—just the thirty pieces I had created for myself.

So, I incorporated, and Jordan Alexander Jewelry was born.

No business, especially a start-up, is easy. It was 2008 at the height of the banking crisis, the worst time to start a fine jewelry business, but we came out of the gate strong. For the first few years, the press drove the business. My designs were featured on many celebrities and in most major fashion magazines. From *Harper's Bazaar* to *Oprah, Elle, Robb Report,* and *Vogue,* and were seen on Julia Roberts, Pink, Jennifer Hudson, Oprah, and the list goes on.

I worked hard to learn manufacturing fundamentals, develop inventory control systems, source pearls and stones, staff the business, and train a team. Designing was never hard, and coming up with new ideas was never hard. But, running a business in which I had no experience? That was hard.

I knew the rapid expansion and impressive publicity I was experiencing in the jewelry business was highly unusual, but sadly, I didn't have time to savor it.

I was also running a sizable marketing company at the same time. Truthfully, that was my downfall.

I was so consumed with managing two businesses and leading the creative efforts in both that I didn't see what was happening right under my nose.

For two years, a trusted employee and friend I had hired for a key position in the jewelry company had committed fraud. By the time it surfaced, it was massive.

It was a devastating betrayal that shattered the deep bonds of friendship and trust I had built around my business—a business that was not only my livelihood but my passion. The fraud brought everything crashing down, leaving me reeling.

In the middle of this turmoil, as I grappled with debt and sought ways to salvage what I could, James passed away.

When James died, any resolve I had left crumbled; a torrent of emotions engulfed me — confusion, grief, and a profound loss of self-confidence. Each day was a struggle to merely think clearly, much less envision any kind of future.

Unable to see a way to sustain the business and pay off the mounting debt, I made the difficult decision to close it.

And then the shame came.

It did not come in little bits and pieces or in a whisper; I became weighted and shrouded in layers and layers of shame.

The thing about shame is that it's the last thing you want to share. You can admit grief; it's expected, but shame is buried deep and feels like the darkest of secrets.

It was more than the failure of the business. It shook a core part of my belief system. I'd always told myself that being an artist meant I could do anything creative—whether it was music, painting, filmmaking, or designing jewelry, it all flowed from the same place inside me. It's more vulnerable than I want to say, but somehow, by following my instincts, I was good at designing jewelry. It felt like this incredible, almost magical place inside me had come alive, pouring out designs that people loved, and the press praised. That's what made it cut so much deeper when I lost the business. I didn't just lose a company—I lost an entire avenue for creating, for expressing that part of myself that could make something truly special. It was like losing a piece of my soul.

I was covered in shame — for disappointing the people who had believed in me and invested in the business. My success stood on the shoulders of stores faithful to the brand and who had worked hard to sell my designs. I had assembled a core team of people who worked tirelessly alongside me to make the business successful. It was heartbreaking to disappoint them and leave them without jobs. My investors were also close friends. They believed in the business and me. I had let them down. It was gut-wrenching. I felt I had failed all the good people who had cared about me and the business.

The journey of creating that amazing business was one of the highest highs of my life and now one of the lowest lows.

I had never encountered that kind of failure before. There was a myriad of emotions — sadness, worry, anger, immense shame, self-doubt, and deep disappointment.

New York Times bestselling author, Brene Brown says three things keep you from the path of healing, "…Secrecy, shame, and judgment."

In the first months, I sat squarely in the middle of all three.

I was holding all the unknowns of James' suicide as an impenetrable secret.

As I said earlier, real or perceived, I felt such deep judgment about his suicide. A few people along the way were so unthoughtful as to ask, "Didn't you know something was going on with him?" "Wasn't there something you could have done?" I wanted to gut-punch them. They had no idea of the hurt, the sorrow, and the confusion I was in. I would have done anything to save him. I would have done anything to get him back.

Feeling judged lights a match to shame. I was on fire with it.

I gradually realized that the shame I carried from the business failure made recovering from the overwhelming sorrow of losing James even harder.

Prayer of Gratitude

I'm grateful for the drive of the creative spirit. I am grateful for twelve years of hard work and some of the best times of my life. I'm grateful for the lessons that failure teaches. Thank you.

Chapter 7

My Kitchen Cabinet

During a conversation about the significance of community with Oprah, Michele Obama poignantly expressed how friendship was the key to surviving the unique pressures of being the First Lady of the United States. She explained how she had a small, close-knit group of "kitchen table people" — a group of women who chose to journey with her, champion her, mentor her, and most importantly, be honest with her. I can't imagine the pressure of being America's First Lady, but in this recent season of loss and grief, I found myself deeply resonating with her observation, "It's a rare thing to have one die-hard friend you can do life with. It's a gift from heaven to have a table full of them." Frankly, I'm not sure I would've survived without them.

In the discombobulating immediate aftermath of James' death, I didn't have the bandwidth to be intentional about a "kitchen table of friends," but God graciously rallied the right people to fill the chairs around my broken heart.

You will often hear me speak about my sister, Lisa Harper — truly a force of nature. She's one of the strongest yet most tender-hearted people I know, undoubtedly the funniest person in our family, while I got all the seriousness.

In the initial months after James died, Lisa's kindness was boundless.

I was a broken record with my shame and pain, but she was patient. She was what I like to call a 'generous listener.'

She sprinkled our conversations with tiny bits of hope, subtle hints at things that might help me. With all her heart, she worked to guide me out of my deep sorrow and despair, offering a nurturing perspective on when we fail in life and when life falls apart.

Lisa began to heal the raw edges of my grief and became a lifeline I clung to.

And she prayed for me.

There were days when she would call, and all I could do was cry at the other end of the phone. I couldn't absorb her words or suggestions, but I didn't want her to hang up, so she would start praying. Gentle words, encouraging words, words of healing, words that gave me a tether to her and God. In a subtle way that I didn't realize then, she connected my grief to my spiritual life.

Whatever you choose to call it—God, Spirit, the Universe—I believe we are all guided by a deep, inherent connection to something greater than ourselves. My own belief system is rooted in Christianity, but I also deeply respect and honor the spiritual practices and beliefs of many other faiths. To me, a connection to Spirit is universal, transcending any specific religion. It is what ultimately leads and shapes our lives.

During the most intense period of my grief, I found myself both questioning God and feeling His presence in ways that seemed contradictory. It was a time of deep conflict, where I was angry, full of despair, and not at all polite in my questioning. I wrestled with God, demanding answers, crying out in my pain. But even in that turmoil, I never felt abandoned. In fact, it was in those darkest moments that I sensed Him the most— walking beside me, even carrying me. My questioning didn't diminish His presence; if anything, made it more real.

Lisa continually guided me toward a kind and faithful God, who heard my cries and cried with me. She didn't need to say it outright, but through her gentle presence and unwavering support, she helped me see that my suffering was shaping my spiritual growth. In every conversation, every quiet moment, she reflected on the truth that even in my pain, I was being molded and deepened in ways I hadn't realized. Her compassion was a silent reminder that God was with me, not just as a distant figure but as a tender companion in my journey.

She was right. Over the last five years, my sorrow and pain have motivated me to seek spiritual practices that help me navigate through grief, fear, and anxiety. Prayer has always come naturally to me. It's been a part of my life since I was a child, and I still pray throughout my days, but my prayers have changed; they are deeper and more intentional. I've also embraced a daily meditation practice that combines prayer with intention, breathing, silence, and listening. This practice has become a vital part of my life. It grounds me.

Another wise friend of mine, Lisa Zimmer, often uses the phrase "Spirit whispers," which has truly been my experience. I've learned to pay attention to those whispers of guidance. I believe we're always being led—by God, the Universe, and our Spiritual connection—but so often, we fail to notice it. In my experience, Spirit doesn't shout or demand our attention; instead,

Spirit whispers, nudging us in the right direction. It's easy to overlook if we're not listening, but I've come to understand that the quietest voices often carry the most profound truths.

I've become much more intentional about listening. And I've found I listen best in stillness. I come away from my mediations and prayers with so much more clarity — sometimes with tangible answers, but always with a shift in perspective that is more positive and hopeful.

Speaking of quiet voices, Marie is another beloved member of my 'Kitchen Cabinet.' My deep friendship with her helped me find my strength and stability. Few friends in life are as faithful and consistent as she has been. From the day James died until this very moment as I'm writing, she has not missed a single day of checking on me, encouraging me, believing in me, and helping me find my way. In those first few months, there were days when I was so angry and broken that I couldn't even bring myself to answer her texts. But she pressed on, never wavering. She has cared for me with a tenderness that is also fierce, and her unwavering support has been a crucial part of the foundation of my survival.

Marie taught me so much about the power of friendship in my grief journey. In her quiet, unassuming way, she made it clear that she would be there for me. Every. Single. Day. No matter what.

It was the early days of COVID, a time when the world seemed to have paused, and isolation was the new normal. There were no coffee dates, no lunches out, or early evening wine times. But week after week, through those long, lonely months, Marie would invite me over to her screened-in porch. We kept our distance, following the new rules, but she was always there, offering me my favorite pimento cheese from Zoe's, gently urging me to eat.

Marie was more than a friend; she was a lifeline. She had known James for all their adult lives and loved him dearly. His death left her devasted and bewildered, yet she somehow knew exactly what I needed. She understood that I had to talk about him— about every part of his life, about the intricacies of our marriage, about the moments that defined us. And I needed to talk about the most painful part— why he chose to die.

Talking about death, especially suicide is something most people shy away from. It's heavy, uncomfortable, and raw. Our culture doesn't have a language to discuss death. Nor do we give the grieving time to grieve. Grief isn't over, and life isn't back to normal in two weeks. Grief is a long, long process.

Marie was different in that regard. She listened with a patience that seemed infinite. She never once made me feel like my grief was too much for her to bear. She left the door wide open, allowing me to walk through it as many times as I needed, and boy, did I need it. Months and months of the same conversations, the same circling around my pain, and she never faltered, never made me feel like I was a burden.

When nothing in my life felt steady, when I thought I had vanished alongside James, Marie's unwavering presence became an anchor. Her consistency and her unyielding support became part of the scaffolding I desperately needed to begin rebuilding my life.

Never underestimate the truth and power of the love of those you trust. It took me a while to open up and let others into my grief, but I eventually realized how essential it was. I needed their love, support, and guidance to navigate the pain; I couldn't do it alone. Trusting others with my sorrow wasn't easy, but it was necessary, and in that vulnerability, I found the strength to begin healing.

There came a time, a few months after James died when I wanted to go back to the lake. I loved that place so much but couldn't make myself go alone. My sweet friend Ginger took many of her Saturday afternoons and early Sunday mornings to meet me there that first summer. We talked for hours and cried through most of it. I loved to paddleboard, and she learned to paddleboard with me.

We had some hysterical moments; I'll never forget trying to teach her to balance her tiny 105-pound body in the middle of the board so she wouldn't turn over. When I thought she had it, I gasped as I watched her fall off the board in one of the most spectacular falls ever. She got so mad because I couldn't stop laughing, and the madder she got, the harder I laughed. Sitting on a paddleboard in the middle of the lake, laughing uncontrollably, was good for my spirit, even if it was the result of Ginger's wildly unpredictable falls!

Ginger had a way of championing me at a core level. She poured positive words of gratitude into me and pushed me out of my blame game. She was also a prayer warrior, calling down heaven with her words of comfort and an unstoppable faith. She's one of the most tenacious women I've ever met. She will not let go when she believes in something—she was determined to pull me out of despair and force-fed me hope.

There were so many things that I didn't know how to do to take care of the lake house. James had made it all seem so easy, but it was the antithesis of that for me. I'll never forget a Saturday morning when Ginger got up and said, "Your lavender is overtaking the yard; it needs pruning." I had no idea how to go about pruning large, old, woody lavender bushes. And I am deathly afraid of snakes. But Ginger wouldn't let me back out of it. We spent a long, hot morning cutting back those bushes. I cried through most of it and sometimes yelled at Ginger because I was so angry about everything I had to do that I didn't know how to, but Ginger kept me moving. There were no snakes; there were, however, lots of mosquitoes and no-see-ums. Poor Ginger was covered with bites when we got through.

During the first year or so after James' death, I didn't consider the pain and grief my friends were going through alongside me. I was so immersed in my sorrow that I couldn't see theirs. But in the years since, I've been able to understand how James' death created immense pain and suffering for all who knew him. My friends and family adored James. They looked up to him as someone to emulate for his kindness, his humility, and his sense of humor. James was a rock for my sister, someone she could count on to care for us all. That was a big trust for her and a devasting loss. I would later hear my friends, and my sister talk about how much they loved James, how shattered they were by his death, and how his death shook parts of their underpinning.

Of course, as I've thought back on those early days of the "Kitchen Table's" selfless care for me, I wish I could have given them more space to grieve alongside me. I don't think I did that, but to a fault, they were generous in their care for me, always putting my pain first. Those acts of love were building blocks for me, helping me *become*. Their consistent compassion effectively laid the stones that established a path for me to walk out of the debilitating pain and shame and start living again. Learning to share my grief and shame with that divinely handpicked handful of friends was integral to my healing. And it has become the necessary scaffolding for the new life I'm building.

It's impossible to overstate how much being in a small, safe community of women means to me. I count on my band of sisters. They come from all walks of life. They don't care about how successful I am, what I wear, or where I live. They care about the state of my heart.

One of the greatest survival tools I've learned is that sharing your pain lessens its power.

Author and theologian Henri Nouwen expresses it far better than I can:

"When we honestly ask ourselves which person in our lives means the most to us, we often find that it is those who, instead of giving advice, solutions, or cures, have chosen rather to share our pain and touch our wounds with a warm and tender hand."

Again, it wasn't easy for me to begin sharing my pain with my friends — self-reliance, which I thought was one of my greatest strengths until it became a hurdle in my healing, made me hesitant to ask for help — but I now believe it is *essential* for restoration. Therefore, I strongly encourage you to find your very own 'Kitchen Table' of family and friends who will journey with you, champion you, and hold you up when you don't have the strength to carry the weight of your own life. They don't have to have answers. The healing comes in sharing your pain.

Prayer of Gratitude

I'm so thankful for the honest, safe friends you sent to pour water on my parched heart. I'm undone by how they held me up when the knees of my heart were too weak to hold my own weight. I'm beyond grateful for the power of human connection and how it heals us. Thank you.

Chapter 8

Letting Go

Twenty-three years ago, a saint named Adiela joined our family to help with the boys, who were four and eight years old at the time. She quickly became a beloved and integral part of our family's fabric, sharing every milestone of raising two boys and supporting me as I started the jewelry business. When James died, she was by my side every single day. We affectionately call her Adi; she possesses a deep, quiet wisdom. She could sense when I needed encouragement to get out of the house and go for a walk or when sharing some chicken salad and crackers with her might lift my spirits. And she instinctively knew when I couldn't bring myself to leave my bedroom. On those days, she would come in with a cup of coffee or a Diet Coke, saying little, but her presence brought me so much solace.

Over the last five years, I've had the privilege— and, as part of my healing process, the necessity— of speaking with many people who, like me, have experienced the profound loss of a loved one. Invariably, one of the most challenging things we face is dealing with the physical remnants of their lives.

Cleaning out James' closet was a task I dreaded more than

anything after his death. His things—those jackets, the T-shirts, the suits he wore with such elegance, even his worn gardening clothes—weren't just clothes. They were pieces of him, fragments of a life lived thoughtfully and intentionally.

James didn't simply wear clothes; he embodied them. Every item in that closet was carefully chosen; every piece was selected with a discerning eye for quality and an appreciation for artistry.

When I finally found the strength to stand in the doorway of his closet, it felt like he was still there. His leather jackets, lined up by length and color, were more than jackets to me; they were memories of laughter-filled Saturdays, spontaneous dates, and mountain getaways. Each garment, made of ordinary fabric and thread, was a portal to a moment in time, a tangible link to the man I loved.

I told Adi that I wanted to keep some of his sweaters; she understood without a word or a questioning look. She walked into the closet and, with the same care James would have shown, selected a few sweaters, folded them tenderly, and placed them in my drawer.

In the raw, agonizing months following his death, I clung to those sweaters. They became a ritual, a lifeline. After a day of work, I would slip into one of his sweaters, seeking comfort in the familiar scent, the faint echo of his presence. In those quiet moments, it felt as though he was still with me, not just in spirit but almost physically. The sweaters were my way of holding onto him, of keeping him close when everything else felt so distant.

In some inexplicable way, my mind clung to the illusion that James wasn't really gone. Every time I pulled on one of his sweaters, it was as if I were waiting for him to walk through the door, ready to slip back into our evening routine—sharing stories, cooking together, and unwinding from the day. I wanted so desperately to believe that he was still alive, that life could still hold the warmth of his presence.

I couldn't bring myself to part with his ties, that remarkable collection that he wore with such confidence and style. But deep down, I knew I had to share a part of him with those who loved him so dearly. So, I decided to gift his ties, one by one, to his closest friends; I wrapped each one with care like I was handing over a piece of his soul. And when those friends later told me how they wore his ties to important presentations or special meetings, and how they felt his presence as if he were standing beside them, urging them on with his quiet strength, I felt both the ache of loss and the comfort of knowing he was still touching lives.

It was Adi who helped me with the unbearable task of cleaning out his closet. I know it wasn't easy for her—James was so much more than an employer; he was someone she deeply respected, someone who had been a steady presence in her life. She trusted him, leaned on him, and he protected her too.

When I was finally ready to let go, Adi took on the heartbreaking duty of sorting through his clothes. I watched her fold each piece with such reverence, placing them in bags and bins as if she were preparing him for one final journey. For her, it wasn't a task; it was a way of saying goodbye, of caring for him one last time.

How do you describe a friend like that? Words fall short. Adi didn't only walk beside me in my grief; she bore it with me. She mourned with me, and when I couldn't stand, she held me up. She was more than a friend — she was integral to my survival.

One of the most challenging places for me to let go of was

our home, especially since it carried memories of our early years together. Not long after James and I were married, we built a house about thirty minutes from town, tucked away with a breathtaking view of the mountains. The location wasn't ideal—it didn't fit into our day-to-day lives of school runs, work, or seeing friends—but we fell in love with what we could afford. The view was our dream, and in those early days, we had no idea how life would unfold. We told ourselves we'd only stay there for three or four years. But as it turned out, that house, with all its inconveniences, became the perfect place to raise our boys.

We had two acres, and at the bottom of the property was a small river, the Cahaba. It took several years, but when James found the time, he gradually built a tree house near the river. It became the boys' kingdom and freedom for them and their friends, starting when they were in kindergarten.

Weekends were rarely quiet. There were always kids running through the house, laughing and playing. James loved making homemade swords so they could imagine themselves as heroes from *Star Wars*—Han Solo, Obi-Wan Kenobi, or Darth Vader—locked in epic battles.

The mountainside of the property was their fortress, the perfect setting for airsoft gun wars as they aged. These made them feel like conquerors of their own world.

As the boys grew, we transformed the basement into a playroom. Football became a ritual in our home when they became interested in sports. James and the boys watched game after game, but nothing brought more energy than cheering on Alabama college football. We talked about coach Nick Saban as though he was part of our family.

Our open kitchen flowed into the den, creating a space

where we gathered as a family, where the sounds of football yells and cheers echoed. James was always within arm's reach in the kitchen, grilling burgers, ribs, hotdogs, and Italian sausages, filling the air with smells that still make my heart ache with nostalgia. It was a house full of life, and it held everything that mattered most to us.

The house we thought we'd only stay in for a few years became the heart of our family, a place we grew to treasure deeply. We welcomed our second child during our first year there, and it quickly became the backdrop for every holiday, birthday, and lazy Sunday afternoon. It wasn't just a house—it was a sanctuary where we built our lives, learning to be the best parents we knew how to be, giving our children a sense of safety and a home they could always return to.

James and I grew there, too, as a couple, through all the ups and downs of life. By the time James passed away, we had lived in that house for twenty-three years. It was the only home I'd known as an adult, and its walls felt thick with the memories, secrets, and love that held our family together.

Despite the challenges we faced—because no marriage or family is without them—James and I were so proud of what we'd built. Our boys grew into good human beings, and no matter what life threw at us, we never lost sight of the fact that we still enjoyed each other. We loved spending time together. There was always this quiet trust between us, knowing that no matter what, we had each other's backs. Love and respect were the foundation of everything we did.

For two and a half years after James died, I couldn't bring myself to think about selling the house. His death shattered me, and I didn't have the strength to make such a huge change. The house was far too big for me to live in alone, but it felt like leaving would mean leaving behind the life we had, leaving what was left of him.

It's not rational, but grief rarely is. Some part of me clung to the idea that if I stayed, he was still there with me. For months after he died, I would expect to hear him come through the door in the evening or find him in the kitchen, making dinner when I got home.

My heart still waited for him, even though my mind knew better. It's the cruelest trick grief plays—your heart refuses to catch up with the reality that the person you love is gone.

Every day was a painful reminder of his absence. I would turn the corner expecting to see him, only to be met with an empty room. I would come home, eager to share my day, only to realize no lights were on and no one was there.

The daily things, the ordinary moments, became the most excruciating reminder of loss.

One of my dearest friends, Laura, knew exactly what I was going through, even without me saying it. Laura has been a part of my life almost as long as James had, and she intuitively understood the pain of staying in that house.

She's a brilliant interior designer, and a few months after James died, she visited me. I was sitting on the sofa in the den off the kitchen, where James and I used to sit every night to talk or watch TV.

Without directly addressing the obvious, she gently suggested that we freshen up the house a little, asking if she could bring over a few things to brighten my space.

She brought a new sofa, rearranged some furniture, and made the room feel less overwhelming with memories. In her quiet wisdom, she was helping me take those first small steps toward letting go, even though, at the time, I didn't fully understand it.

Over the next two years, she kept nudging me in small ways, encouraging me to clear out a closet here and a storage room there. It was never easy, but slowly, she helped me begin the process of making the house a little lighter, easier to live in, and without my realizing it, easier to leave.

Eventually, I put the house on the market two and a half years after James' death. It sold quickly, and I found myself faced with the enormous task of packing up twenty-five years of life. I had to sort through everything the boys had left behind when they went off to college, and I had to pack away every trace of the life I had built with James. It sent me into a tailspin, making me feel like all the progress I thought I had made in my grief had crumbled beneath me. The suffering, loss, fear, and anger came crashing down all over again.

As I sorted through my feelings, I understood how leaving or selling a home after a loved one dies often feels like a repetition of that loss. The memories in those spaces anchor us to them in a way that is so hard to let go of.

C.S. Lewis, a renowned Christian theologian and writer, discusses the pain of loss and the emotional connection to the space our loved one inhabited.

"The death of a beloved is an amputation...for in grief nothing 'stays put.' One keeps on emerging from a phase, but it always recurs. Round and round. Everything repeats."

That's exactly how I felt as I began packing up the house. My early grief felt like it was on repeat.

Once again, Adi quietly and calmly helped me find my way. She knew which parts of the house would be the most difficult for me to pack, so she tried to organize them for me to pack in little bits, not all at once. Truthfully, it's been two and a half years since I moved, and I'm still unable to unpack the photos of James that had been scattered around the house or the things that were in his office. One day, I'll be strong enough, but I'm still not there.

However, I understand my thoughts and feelings much more clearly these days. I feel that it's essential for me to say that losing someone we love to suicide is a heartbreak that defies words. The grief that follows is not only filled with sorrow but also deep confusion, guilt, and a sense of helplessness that can feel unbearable. We are left with so many unanswered questions, and there's so much we wish we could have said or done differently. It's a wound that cuts deeper than most because we feel as though their pain slipped through our fingers, and we couldn't stop it.

Letting go of someone we've lost this way is not just about accepting their absence but grappling with the complexity of their suffering. We often carry the burden of their choice, replaying memories, wondering how we missed the signs or if we could have loved them more or better.

It's a grief that comes in waves— sometimes with anger, sometimes with overwhelming sadness, and sometimes with the sharp sting of guilt.

But as much as we ache, letting go doesn't mean forgetting them or dismissing their struggles. Letting go means finding a way to honor their lives while understanding that we couldn't carry their pain for them. It means embracing our own healing, step by step, even when it feels impossible.

In time, we learn to carry their memory with tenderness

rather than despair, recognizing that their decision wasn't a reflection of our love or their lack of it but of a battle they could no longer fight.

In the last five years, I've learned that letting go is not about abandoning James—it's about finding peace with myself while holding on to the love that will always be there.

Prayer of Gratitude

Thank you for time, because, as the adage says, it allows for healing. Thank you for the strength to let go of what doesn't allow me to heal while still holding space for a love that will always be.

Chapter 9

Acceptance

As I began to let go of some of the material things that made up my life with James, there was still a part of me clinging to the hope—irrational as it might seem—that he would somehow return. It's one of the strange tricks the mind plays in the wake of grief, this refusal to fully accept what has happened. I kept looking for my life to normalize, for some sign that this was all a bad dream. Deep down, I wanted to believe that life could still go back to the way it was before.

But learning to accept, in the quietest and deepest parts of my being, that he was not coming back and that life as I had known it was over—was a long and grueling process.

Acceptance didn't happen all at once. It wasn't an epiphany or even a linear journey. It came in fragments, in fits and starts, usually when I least expected it.

Every time I thought, "I am beginning to move forward," another layer of grief would pull me back, forcing me to confront the enormity of what I had lost all over again.

What made it even harder was realizing that accepting his death wasn't just about acknowledging that he was gone. It was about understanding that my entire life had shifted in ways I couldn't control. The world I had built with him—our routines, our shared dreams, the future we had planned—was gone. I had to stop waiting for some magical moment when things would click back into place. There was no going back.

Emotionally, this realization was hard. It unraveled me. At first, I fought it. I clung to my work, my routines, the things that felt familiar. Over time I began to see that my resistance wasn't helping me heal—it was keeping me stuck. I was beginning to see that if I wanted to survive this, I had to let go of the life I thought I would have and make space for whatever might come next.

Mentally, this shift required a new level of awareness. I had to start paying attention to the stories I was telling myself; I had to stop replaying the "what-ifs" and imagining alternate endings where James was still here. Instead, I began to focus on what I could do with the life I had now. I started asking myself questions that felt daunting at first: What do I want for my life moving forward? What kind of person do I want to become through this? How can I find meaning in this pain?

Those questions became my guideposts, even when I didn't have answers. They helped me shift my perspective from one of helplessness to one of possibility. I was ever so slowly making peace with reality so that I could move forward.

I made a lot of mistakes along the way. One that stands out was the first time I decided to go hiking again. As you know from previous chapters, hiking had been such a huge part of my life with James—it was something we loved deeply and shared often. It wasn't just a hobby; it was woven into the fabric of who we were as a couple. So, when a girlfriend of mine, an avid hiker, invited me to Montana for a five-day trip, I jumped at the chance. I thought it might help me reconnect with something I had lost and give me a sense of myself again.

The hikes were beautiful, of course, Montana's vast skies and rugged landscapes were breathtaking. But the truth is, they took more out of me than they gave. Physically, the hikes were exhausting, but the emotional weight undid me. Being there without James, walking trails that reminded me of all the adventures we'd shared was devastating in ways I hadn't anticipated. Hiking had always been a source of joy and connection for me, but on this trip, it didn't feel at all that way.

The reality of going on trips with a girlfriend instead of James hit me hard. The easy rhythm I had shared with James on the trail, the quiet moments when we didn't need to speak, and the shared sense of accomplishment at the summit—all of that was missing. Instead, I was acutely aware of how different everything felt.

I didn't want to believe this was what my life would look like now—that this was the only way I could see the world, through the lens of what was missing. It tore me up inside to see that this was my new reality, that no matter how hard I tried, nothing could feel the way it once had. I left Montana feeling more broken than before, realizing just how much grief could follow me.

I couldn't keep chasing the life I had with James. The hikes, the adventures, the moments I thought would bring me comfort— they couldn't. Not in the way I wanted. I realized I was trying to force my old life to fit into my new reality, and it wasn't working.

That trip underscored that grief wasn't something I could outrun, and it wasn't something I could erase by trying to recreate old memories. Grief was going to come with me, no matter where I went, and I had to live with it and accept it.

That trip to Montana wasn't the only time I felt the sharp, disorienting contrast between the life I'd had with James and the one I was trying to build without him. Being a single mother, after years of the partnership James and I had shared as parents, was so hard for me.

Andrew moved to New Jersey for graduate school a year after James died. I was so proud of him, of course, but the first time I visited him in his new life, the reality of my own hit me in a way I wasn't prepared for. James should have been there. The two of us should have been together, marveling at how our son had grown into this independent, brilliant young man. Instead, it was just me. I'd go to dinner with Andrew, talk and laugh, and do my best to be fully present, but the minute I closed the door to my hotel room, I would collapse into sobs. The loneliness and its permanence were overwhelming.

I wanted to be an example of strength and hope for Andrew and Jordan, but I didn't feel strong in my private moments. I was barely holding it together.

And then there was sweet Jordan. I remember the first time I went to his house for dinner after James died. I had never been there without James, and walking through the door felt like stepping into a memory that had been edited, with James removed. Jordan and Rachel were so kind—they made the most incredible dinner, creating a safe and welcoming space for me. But the moment I got into my car and started driving home in the dark, I was consumed by the emptiness. There was no one in the car with me, no one to talk to about the evening or share in the pride I felt for the lives our sons were building.

In those moments, being alone in a hotel room in New Jersey or driving away from Jordan's house alone, I began to grasp the magnitude of what it meant to parent without James. I was the sole anchor for my boys, the only parent. I missed James beyond any words I could come up with.

I understood that being a strong mother didn't mean pretending I had it all together. It meant showing up even when I didn't know how to be for those boys what their father had been. I was deeply grieving James in every corner of my life. But I had no choice other than to go on and do the best I could to love my boys well, even though I couldn't be both mother and father.

Ultimately, my vulnerability and unsureness created a tender space between us; there was no pretense, and the honesty was unfiltered. I could see that my boys were trying, in their ways, to open up to me and make room for me to nurture them the best way I knew now. They didn't expect me to step into the enormous role James had played in their lives, and perhaps that freed us all to meet each other in this uncharted in-between space, pretending to be anything other than what we were: a grieving family, searching for balance in a world that was unrecognizable.

I began to see the unexpected beauty of how they were navigating our new reality. They grew in ways I hadn't anticipated. They became much more patient, empathetic, and willing to lean into the complexities of what we were facing. Their kindness toward me sometimes felt boundless, and I saw how they made room for my grief. And I changed in the process as well. I was no longer the mother who always knew what to do but a person fumbling forward, learning how to rebuild from the ground up. I think they started to see me not just as their mother but also as a grieving woman trying with all of her being to rebuild her life.

I'm not sure we realized what was slowly rising between us,

but it was a deeper connection, a closeness beyond what we had known before. What grew in the space left by the loss was a tenderness that bound us in a way I will forever cherish.

Anne Roiphe, who wrote *Epistles: A Memoir of Grief,* poignantly stated, "Grief is in two parts. The first is loss. The second is the remaking of life."

That was and still is the journey I'm on, continuing to hold the grief I feel for the loss of James and often stumbling and falling while trying to remake my life.

As I slowly began to accept this new truth, this new path of going forward alone, another truth became clear: there were some questions I would never have answers to. For months, I replayed every conversation I'd had with James, parsing through every nuance of his last days, trying to understand why he hadn't let me in during his darkest moments. I searched for clues, for signs I might have missed. I tortured myself with the "what if" and "if only," as if I could rewrite the past by analyzing it enough.

I finally came to a point when I realized I could spend the rest of my life searching for answers and still never find them. James' death was a puzzle I couldn't solve. The choice I faced wasn't whether to understand it—it was whether to let it consume me or to release it and find a way to live with the unknown.

Accepting the unknowable wasn't easy. It felt like giving up on something I desperately wanted to make sense of. Over time, I began to see it a little differently. Letting go of the need for answers didn't mean I stopped caring or stopped grieving—it meant I was making space for life again.

Acceptance permitted me to focus on the parts of my story that I could shape. Instead of being stuck in the loop of unanswerable questions, I started asking new ones: "What do I want my life to look like now? How can I carry James' memory with me while creating a future he would want me to live?

In accepting that I was moving forward alone and that I would never truly understand the *why* behind James' death, I began to uncover feelings of unexpected gratitude. I felt grateful for the deep and honest conversations I was having with my boys—conversations we never would have had without the loss we all shared. I saw their resilience strengthening, and their strength shored up mine.

I was also grateful for the deepening friendships around me. In my willingness to be seen—truly seen—at my most broken and vulnerable, others found the courage to meet me in my brokenness. My friendships were and still are a source of profound comfort, their honesty a balm for my soul.

Strangely, I even found gratitude in the pain itself. The intensity of my grief was a testament to how deeply I had loved. To miss James so fiercely, to feel his absence in every breath, was to know that I had experienced a love so rare and profound it was worth every ounce of the heartache it left behind.

Acceptance became my bridge. It connected the early days of unimaginable grief and sorrow to the unfolding reality of my life—the life I was slowly choosing to rebuild. Through the lens of acceptance, I began to see that the end of one chapter didn't mean the end of the book. The story wasn't over, and I wasn't done living it.

I began to honor the pieces of my life that remained. In that honoring, I gave myself permission to dream—not of replacing what had been but of creating something new from the ashes of what had been.

Hope didn't rush in; it came in quietly. Acceptance allowed me to acknowledge the depth of my grief but also the growing depth of my resilience. It wasn't about forcing myself to be strong or pretending I had everything figured out. It was about making peace with what I didn't know and what I couldn't change, and trusting that even without all the answers, I could still take the next step.

I slowly began to imagine a new life—I'm still imagining it. It does not replace what I've lost; rather, it builds on what I've learned through the journey of grief and loss.

Prayer of Gratitude

I am so grateful for the lessons of acceptance, which taught me that healing is not about erasing pain but about learning to carry it with grace. Thank you for showing me that loss does not diminish love; it deepens it and leaves a legacy of connection that endures beyond the physical.

Thank you for the resilience that has quietly grown in my heart. I am grateful for the vulnerability that has softened me, allowing me to connect with others in ways I never imagined.

I am also grateful for the mysteries I cannot unravel and for the unanswered questions that remind me to trust in the unknown. Thank you that I don't need to have all the answers to have peace.

Chapter 10

Transforming Fear into Courage

Throughout this book, I've mentioned my boys often, but I haven't shared much about their journey of survival after losing their dad. You might wonder why I've been vague about how they've navigated life after such a profound loss. When I told them I was writing this, they asked me not to share their stories, and I deeply respect that. Their journey is theirs alone to tell, not mine. That said, my survival is integrally linked to my relationships with my boys. So, I will tell you about them in terms of how they loved, guided, and helped me heal.

In the first days and months after James passed away, there was a constant unspoken fear running through all of us: that we'd never be the family we once were, that we'd never find happiness or normalcy again.

Every memory felt like a painful echo of when James was with us, and every day was heavy with the reminder of what we had lost. It was an uncertain time when the future felt too empty to face. We were each carrying our grief differently, but our shared loss held us together even though we weren't sure how to go on.

When James passed away, neither Andrew nor Jordan was married, though both were in relationships with powerful yet gentle women—women who are now their wives.

I vividly remember the day James died. I sat outside his office for five long hours, waiting for the coroner to release his body.

In those hours, I realized that every action I took from that moment onward would be etched into my sons' memories forever: the way I broke the news to them about their father and how I carried myself in those initial, excruciating days would set the tone for how we might begin to heal as a family.

Looking back, I marvel at how I found the strength to think so clearly. Something within me came forward, allowing me to push through the unimaginable and put my children first. That strength held me together in those early crucial moments, though I would later collapse under the weight of grief, as you know.

For the past five years, I have set my heart on being there for them, supporting their healing however I could. But in truth, it's been the other way around—they have been my greatest source of healing, lifting me in ways I couldn't have imagined.

At just 22 and 26, they were still so young, barely men, when James died. I doubt they ever imagined that something could shatter life as they knew it, the way his suicide tore apart the very fabric of our family they had always relied on.

Andrew had just been accepted to graduate school and planned to move after the summer, while Jordan was deeply immersed in his work, building a career.

Gabrielle, Andrew's girlfriend, was still new to our lives—I had met her just the Christmas before. But as parents do, I knew immediately that she was extraordinary.

When I reflect on those first days after James's death, I can't help but wonder how that tender, beautiful twenty-two-year-old girl managed to cope with the immense sorrow that came crashing into her life simply because she was part of Andrew's world—and by extension, part of mine.

Looking back on those early months, I tenderly remember the quiet comfort she brought to our lives. She regularly visited our house, bringing a gentle, grounding presence that felt like a lifeline. She would rise early every morning, make coffee, and share a quiet conversation with me before the day began. She was such a source of encouragement to me.

Gabrielle brought much-needed warmth into our home through her incredible baking. She would fill the kitchen with the comforting smells of cakes, bread, and pastries that made the house feel alive again. There's something deeply soothing about the scent of freshly baked treats that transforms a house into a home, and Gabrielle's baking did just that. The aroma would drift through the rooms, wrapping us in a cozy sweetness that softened the ache of grief. We'd gather around her creations, too eager to wait until they'd cooled, reaching for warm slices and bites from the oven. Her baking became a source of comfort; love poured out.

Through those most challenging days of my grief, when it felt like I was breaking in half with sobs, she was there without judgment, never once making me feel like my sorrow was too much. Her maturity was astounding— she carried decades of wisdom within her young heart.

One of the most beautiful things I've ever witnessed was her understanding and tenderness toward Andrew. She held him through his heartbreak as though she had known the depths of love and loss herself. I imagine she had her own dark nights, grieving for the life she thought she'd have, yet each day, she gave us every ounce of her empathy and kindness.

Gabrielle became family, a constant and precious part of our lives. I quickly understood why Andrew had fallen in love with her, and I, too, came to love her deeply as though she were my daughter. She became one of my treasured and most trusted places of solace.

Jordan and Rachel are one of those rare couples who met in high school and are still inseparable fourteen years later. Now married, their bond has only deepened.

I first met Rachel when she was just 16, and even then, she had the drive and tenacity of someone twice her age. From those early days, I admired and mentored her, never guessing she would one day become Jordan's wife.

Like me, Rachel came from a challenging background, but she has steadily overcome each barrier that could have held her back with a strength few could imagine. Now, she's a CPA at one of the country's largest firms— a testament to her resilience.

Along the way, Rachel worked for me in various roles, first at Jordan Alexander Jewelry. It was there that I got to know her. At just 19, her work ethic was unparalleled; she was always the first to arrive and the last to leave. She brought a quiet sweetness to every day, often looking out for me during times of intense business stress. Despite the pressures of the business, Rachel— still so young—was usually the only one on the team checking on me, ensuring I was okay in the whirlwind of being a designer and business owner.

When James passed away, I was left untangling the financial complications caused by fraud at Jordan Alexander. By then, Rachel was a seasoned accountant at a prominent firm, and I was in no condition to handle the long meetings and paperwork that followed.

During the grueling months of legalities, she never left my side. She guided me through every step, listening patiently as I grieved both James and the loss of that beloved business. No matter how often I called in distress, Rachel never made me feel like a burden. She'd greet me with a tight hug, a comfort no words could match. Her unwavering belief in me held me up when I didn't think I could keep going.

Rachel was equally devoted to Jordan. She became his anchor, carrying his pain and quietly supporting him as he navigated his father's loss. Her fierce determination to stand by him through the darkest days left an indelible mark on my heart. If I hadn't already loved her, I would have fallen in love with her then, for the way she cared so deeply for my son.

Four and a half years after James' passing, Rachel and Jordan married quietly and on their terms. I felt James' presence, knowing he would have been so proud of them.

Rachel and Jordan's love is a legacy of resilience, a reminder that love can thrive even in the face of tragic loss.

Immediately after James died, Jordan and Andrew became pillars of strength and compassion for me, showing a selflessness that took my breath away. Though they were both profoundly grieving their father, they always seemed to put my needs first, sensing my heartbreak in a way that only those who share a lifetime of love can. Their presence comforted me beyond words and helped me find a way through the devastation.

It was as if they instinctively knew that their support of me would be instrumental in our family's healing. Jordan, who has always been quiet and strong, would often sit with me, not needing to say anything but letting his presence speak volumes.

I'll never forget a conversation I had with him just a week after his dad died. At that moment, he spoke with wisdom and insight that took me by surprise, reflecting deeply on the pain James had carried and the struggles he had endured. With gentle clarity, he helped me move past the endless question of "why" and into a place of quiet understanding. That conversation shifted something inside me; instead of being anchored in sorrow, we began to talk about honoring James' memory by embracing the love and incredible kindness he had instilled in us.

Jordan and James shared a special bond over movies, watching and dissecting films together for countless hours. Each recommendation from James was more than just a movie—it was his way of sharing life lessons and glimpses into his heart. After James passed, Jordan told me he often realized in hindsight what his dad had been trying to say to him through those films. In a profoundly bittersweet tribute to their connection, he created a list of the 100 movies they had watched together, each title a piece of his father's wisdom and love. It was his way of keeping those cherished memories alive, honoring the legacy of their conversations that had shaped him in ways only he could understand.

Andrew has always had such a tender heart, and in those first overwhelming waves of grief, he did everything he could to ease my pain; he offered comfort in a hundred quiet ways, sensing the depths of my sorrow as deeply as he felt his own. He and James had been inseparable for years, texting and meeting for weekly lunches in Tuscaloosa while Andrew was in school. They shared a bond rooted in understanding and mutual respect, and I know losing his dad left an ache that words could never fully capture; I'll never forget the look in Andrew's eyes for months afterward, filled with unbearable sadness.

But Andrew didn't turn away from his grief. He bravely faced it, letting me into his pain, his tears, and his questions. He stayed with me in my sorrow, creating a space where I could cry freely without ever feeling the need to hide my feelings.

He worried about me, knowing how much I'd relied on James to prepare meals. He began cooking dinner for us every night, just as his dad always did. It must have been so difficult for him, a poignant way to fill the space James had left, but he did it with such care. In his own way, he was trying to give me back pieces of his dad.

Both boys offered an incredible, unspoken gift: a willingness to let me feel everything without trying to fix it. They supported and loved me and allowed me to be raw and vulnerable. That probably wasn't easy for them as my children, who were used to seeing me as a strong woman and a problem solver. Not only had they lost their dad, but in my early grief, I was not the Mom they were used to.

Even though they were both dealing with their own sorrow, they were selfless in their care for me. Each in his own way quietly turned our family's path from despair to hope.

What Jordan and Andrew did for me in those early days allowed us to eventually find a path toward healing. They paved the way for a new life that was to come, reminding me that we could still find a way forward—together.

They comforted me and very gently nudged me toward a place of courage. They set an example of how we could care for each other so we would not have to bear the weight alone. This amalgam of love—theirs, Rachel's, Gabrielle's, and mine—became the heartbeat of our family, stitching us back together one day at a time.

The four of them showed me that love was enduring even through the darkest grief. In that love, we began to find ourselves again.

In his book *On Finding Meaning Amid Suffering*, Viktor Frankl states, "In some ways, suffering ceases to be suffering at the moment it finds a meaning, such as the meaning of a sacrifice."

The support and love of my boys became, for me, the meaning that Frankl suggested. They turned our tragedy into a time of beautiful compassion and courage.

Jordan and Andrew taught me that love can be redefined. We will never be the same family we were before, but we can become something else—something equally as strong, loving, and, I think, more resilient.

Gabrielle and Rachel were unwaveringly there, grounded and constant. Those incredible young women brought a renewed sense of hope to our family. We began to let go of the belief that joy was a thing of the past and started to trust that happiness, in a new way, could still be part of our lives.

It meant creating something new with each other—an act of courage that was as much about honoring James as it was about moving forward. Every moment we spent supporting each other, listening to each other, and urging each other to embrace a new life was a testament to the love James had given all of us.

We began to laugh again, finding joy in small things. We learned that sharing James's fun and funny memories honored him and felt like growth for us.

Eventually, the heavy grief transformed into something gentler, something we could carry without the early feelings of fear. The sorrow didn't disappear, but it softened.

Together, we've come to understand that our family didn't

end with James' death. Instead, it has given us the courage to redefine what it means to be a family, creating a new story that honors the past and is full of promise for all that is still to come.

Prayer of gratitude

There are no words to express my gratitude for my sweet boys and their precious wives. I am blessed beyond measure that those four amazing humans are my family.

Chapter 11

Becoming

I love the word "becoming." A therapist I worked with once explained that as we work through the things that hold us back from living a full and happy life, we *become* who we are meant to be. I began to cling to the idea of working toward *becoming* the woman I wanted to see in the mirror. I realized I had a choice: I could either stay with what was left of my life after James or start finding my way forward into a new life of my own making.

As I write this chapter, it is the tail end of Autumn — that space in nature between endings and beginnings. It reminds me of the beauty of transition, of process, of becoming.

The end of autumn is analogous to the transitions I began to make in my life. I felt pulled to live in a way that aligned with a new purpose bubbling up within me. I couldn't define the purpose, but I knew it was very different from the life I had lived for most of my adult life.

As I started to claw my way out of the depths of grief, I found myself longing for something more than just survival. I wanted my boys to see that this tragedy wouldn't defeat me; it could be the spark for something transformative. I wanted them to witness not just a mother coping but a woman who embodied resilience, who was brave enough to grow through the pain and emerge on the other side with a heart softened by compassion and strengthened by courage. I wanted them to see that even in the darkest valleys, we can discover an inner strength we never knew we had.

Grief had reshaped me at my core. So much of what I once valued now felt hollow, like the shadows of a life I no longer recognized. Success, career, accolades, the rush of professional achievement —I found myself reaching for something I couldn't quite name, a yearning to find something deeper.

Dr. Nancy, the therapist James and I leaned on during the final year of his life, often used a word I couldn't quite reconcile—redemption. She told me that this chapter of my life could be one of redemption, but the idea felt so foreign, so heavy with religious connotations, that I didn't know how to apply it to my own life.

What would redemption look like for me, a woman struggling to redefine herself, certainly through my faith as I knew it, but also through something I had yet to discover?

I thought back to that awful Saturday morning when I couldn't reach anyone else, and she came to James' office. She sat with me for hours, her presence anchoring me as I waited for James' body to be released and moved to the funeral home. Redemption wasn't on my mind that day or the days that followed, but survival was. But over time, as the rawness of grief began to soften, I kept coming back to her words. Redemption. Becoming. Was it possible for me? Could I emerge from this tragedy with something meaningful, something that went beyond survival?

That question was the foundation of my spiritual journey. I didn't know it then, but what I was truly searching for wasn't redemption as defined by anyone or anything else. I was searching for a way to become a woman who could survive, someone strong enough to hold the weight of my grief without being crushed by it. I didn't have the answers, but I consciously began to live the questions.

As I gained some distance from the sharp edges of my initial grief, I started to honor my journey in a way I couldn't before. I had become more vulnerable and less guarded. The armor I once carried so tightly around myself was softening. Instead of needing immediate answers about what redemption or healing should look like, I allowed those questions to sit beside me—first as strangers, then slowly as teachers, and eventually as companions.

I have long loved twentieth-century poet Ranier Maria Rilke. In *Letters to a Young Poet*, Rilke reminds us that healing is a journey and encourages us to be patient with the journey of "becoming." Rilke offers profound advice about embracing uncertainty and the unknown aspects of life. He encourages us to have patience with unsolved issues; when faced with uncertainty, he suggests "try to love the questions themselves" and cautions against seeking immediate answers.

I knew Rainer Maria Rilke's words long before my world crumbled, but it wasn't until after James' sudden death that those words became the fiber of my everyday work to embrace the new life that had been thrust on me.

It didn't happen all at once, but slowly, over time, I embraced a spiritual journey that became a foundational shift for everything that followed. It isn't easy to put into words because spiritual growth is so intangible, yet it touches every part of life in almost indescribable ways.

What I can share are the tools and practices that helped me navigate and reshape my reactions to grief, pain, anger, and fear. These tools weren't a quick fix but offered a steady path through difficult emotions, allowing me to reframe my inner experiences.

For example, learning breathwork helped me find space between an emotion and my reaction to it. Rather than being consumed by anger or drowning in sorrow, I learned to sit with those feelings, to observe them, and eventually to let them pass. This practice opened the door to self-compassion and acceptance, which became a new way of understanding and moving through my pain.

As I progressed, I also wrestled with the uncertainty of it all. Spiritual work can feel "out there" because it requires trust in things that aren't easily seen or proven concepts like energy, intuition, or the healing power of presence. Yet, despite this seeming vagueness, the effects were real. Over time, I felt a new calmness and resilience growing within me, not because my life was easier but because my approach to it was evolving.

Those practices opened me up to listen to my inner knowing in ways I hadn't experienced before; instead of feeling swept away by the overwhelming forces of fear and loss, I began to feel grounded — capable of choosing how I responded to my emotions. I could feel myself releasing stored emotions and trauma from my body, which gave me a deeper understanding of all that I had been going through. I also found myself living more in the present moment rather than in all of the emotions surrounding the loss of James.

The daily practices of meditation, prayer, and energy

movement helped me move into a much more peaceful way of approaching my survival. I was learning that peace isn't dependent on external circumstances; over time, the stillness and peace became a refuge — building blocks in my spiritual journey.

For the first time since James' death, I felt like I could finally break free from that all-encompassing grief and move toward something beyond the pain.

At that time, two years after James' death and three years since the loss of the jewelry business, I wasn't exactly in love with my story. I wasn't ready to share it beyond my closest circle, but I could sense that I was growing kinder to myself. I was not hiding from the hard reality of what my life was. I understood, too, that this journey wasn't about arriving at some grand conclusion; it was about stepping forward day by day, reaching for a better self with every little victory over grief.

I began working with a new therapist who introduced me to EMDR (Eye Movement Desensitization and Reprocessing). This technique was invaluable.

It is a type of therapy that helps people process traumatic memories and reduce the distress these memories cause. In simple terms, EMDR guides a person to recall a traumatic event while engaging in a specific set of eye movements, sounds, or taps. This back-and-forth movement is similar to what happens during REM sleep, where the brain naturally processes memories. By focusing on the trauma in a controlled setting while also experiencing these movements, EMDR helps the brain reprocess the memory in a way that reduces its emotional charge.

EMDR has been widely studied and is considered very effective for treating post-traumatic stress disorder (PTSD). Research shows that it can help reduce symptoms of trauma and anxiety relatively quickly compared to traditional talk therapy.

I felt like EMDR rewired my brain in the way I thought about all the trauma that had happened to me. With the help of this therapy, I was able to reshape some of my darkest memories surrounding James' death and learned to think about them without so much fear and anxiety, with more acceptance and less questioning. With each session, I felt myself shifting as though I were slowly shedding layers of grief, allowing lightness to replace the sorrow that had held me captive.

I was tiptoeing into a new life, tracing the edges of what could come next and beginning to understand just how necessary it was to be gentle with myself.

Sometimes, I went backward, swallowed up by the shadows of my perceived failures, wounds, and fears of never moving beyond the past. Gradually, however, I began to believe that loss alone did not define my life.

The blank canvas ahead of me felt like an invitation to imagine something new — something I could paint, one brushstroke at a time.

I often found myself turning to the wisdom of Maya Angelou, whose profound words about *becoming* struck a deep chord within me. She always reminded her readers to take time to sit back and celebrate themselves in the growth process. I had read her work for years but hearing her speak in person just before her death in 2014 was an unforgettable experience.

At a small gathering, I was seated close enough to see every nuance of her expression. Age had rendered her fragile; she had to be guided, almost carried, to her chair. But once she was seated, she radiated an unmistakable strength. She shared stories rich with life's most profound truths for over an hour, each rolling off her tongue like poetry. One story has stayed with me ever since.

Maya spoke of when she was just seven and a half years old, and her mother's boyfriend brutally raped her. She told her grandmother what had happened to her, and the man who raped her was ultimately arrested. Not long after, he was released from jail but was found dead just days later. It was believed that he was kicked to death.

Only a child would believe that her whispered words to her grandmother about the rape could somehow bring death to the man who hurt her. But in her child's mind, fear and guilt mixed, creating a burden too heavy for words; so, she responded in the only way she knew how—retreating into silence. For five long years, she didn't speak a single word.

In Stamps, Arkansas, her silence was misunderstood. People mocked her, called her cruel names, and tried to break the quiet she wrapped herself in. Though mute, she could hear every ugly, demeaning word they threw her way. The silence became her armor, but it also made her an open target. She held her pain close, feeling each insult as deeply as if they'd been physical blows.

Her grandmother, Annie Henderson — whom Maya called 'Momma'—responded with an unyielding love and faith that would shape Maya's entire life.

Every day, Momma would sit little Maya down on a stool, slowly brushing her hair and speaking words that would become woven into Maya's future. Despite Maya's absolute silence, Momma would say, "One day, you will be a teacher. One day, you will be a preacher. One day, you will teach and preach to many nations."

In those quiet moments, Momma planted a seed within

Maya, instilling the belief that she was destined for something big and beautiful, far beyond the pain keeping her mute.

Maya carried those words with her for the rest of her life, tattooed on her heart. Not only did her grandmother's words come true, but Maya Angelou rose to become a voice of wisdom, resilience, and courage, touching millions with her poetry, stories, and truth. During her lifetime, she was awarded fifty honorary degrees. She *became* the woman her grandmother had always known she would be.

When she finished speaking that day, I was guided to her chair, tears streaming down my face. I was overcome by her presence, her stories, her poetry, and her strength, which was palpable despite her fragility. I'll never forget how she took my hand that day, looked into my eyes, and said with quiet confidence, "Honey, you will be fine. You will rise."

Her words felt like foreshadowing, spoken with strength and prediction, as though she already knew something about my future I couldn't glimpse. Little did either of us know that six years later, I would cling to her words to give me courage, to help me survive, and to 'rise'.

Five years into this journey, my blank canvas is no longer empty; it is streaked with bold brushstrokes, each carrying a piece of the pain, hope, and resilience shaping me. There is still a lot of space left to fill, but as Maya Angelou so beautifully said, 'I am rising.' I am becoming the woman I want to see looking back at me in the mirror—the woman I know James saw within me. With each step, I feel myself moving closer to a life that reflects who I am meant to be.

Prayer of Gratitude

Thank you to all of those in my life who have poured positive, prophetic words into me and encouraged me in my process of Becoming. Thank you for the hope and curiosity percolating about what is still to come... thank you for Redemption.

Chapter 12

Radical Compassion

Recently, I flew out of Birmingham, Alabama, heading back to my home in Florida. As I approached the curbside check-in, I saw a familiar face at the kiosk—a man who had often helped James and me with our luggage whenever we returned from trips. His warm, welcoming smile lit up when he saw me. "Hey, how's your husband?" he asked, his voice full of genuine care.

The words I had to say next were like a heavy stone in my chest, "I'm so sorry to tell you, but he passed away a few years ago."

His reaction was immediately heartbreaking. He looked as if the ground had been pulled from beneath him, collapsing to his knees with his head in his hands, tears streaming down his face, he said, "James was the most excellent man I ever met." He recounted how James would always meet me at the airport, often with flowers, a sweet gesture welcoming me home.

As he tried to check in my luggage, he was so shaken that he had to call for help. His hands were trembling, and tears were flowing uncontrollably. Seeing his grief triggered my own, and I couldn't hold back the flood of memories—memories of James' kindness, gentleness, and unwavering thoughtfulness. Here was a man who had only known James peripherally, yet James' light had touched him so deeply that it left an indelible mark.

Before I left, he hugged me tightly, and we both cried, bound together by shared sorrow and the enduring impact of James' life. As I made my way to Atlanta to catch my connecting flight, my tears remained just below the surface. It hurt—oh, how it hurt—to dredge up those memories, to feel the sharp pang of loss all over again. But amid the tears, there was something else— something unexpected.

I felt so much compassion for that sweet man who was grieving James for the first time. Unexpectedly, I also felt compassion for myself, for the journey, for how much I had been through, and how much I had survived.

Though I considered myself compassionate in terms of how I responded to others' pain and suffering, I had not developed a conscious practice of choosing self-compassion.

Why is self-compassion, not the first thing we reach for in our survival journey instead of the last?

When I began to examine it, I realized I've often neglected self-compassion in my life in favor of self-judgment. Judgment is a cruel master. It's like a secret we all carry, something we don't admit or discuss openly, yet it defines much of our lives.

Patricia, a dear friend of mine, radiates joy like few others I've ever met—not because her life has been a smooth, untroubled journey, but precisely because it has been the opposite. She's faced obstacles that would crush most of us, yet she emerged with a heart full of joy. Her childhood and adolescence were marred by unspeakable abuse, a darkness that could have easily swallowed her whole. But Patricia made a choice—a choice not to let the pain define her. Instead of allowing her suffering to become her identity, she built a way out, brick by brick, with joy as her foundation.

Her story is one of extraordinary resilience. From those dark beginnings, Patricia carved out a successful career as a model, actress, and TV host, ultimately becoming a beloved part of *Deal or No Deal* as suitcase number nine. But her true success is not just in what she's accomplished on the outside—it's in how she's learned to thrive on the inside.

Over the past five years, I've sought out people like Patricia, who, like me, have experienced profound tragedy yet have somehow found the tools to survive and thrive.

I like to tease Patricia because she almost bounces with joy. I tell her she is 'Tiger' from *Winnie the Pooh*. She injects positivity, confidence, and open-heartedness wherever she goes; you can feel the energy shift when she's around. One day, we were chatting, and I asked her how it is that she always seems to have so much joy. She responded-that she learned that the most helpful thing she can do to forge her way through difficulties and tragedy, is to be kind to herself— to examine the situation without blame or judgment.

Patricia's life is a testament to the powerful survival tool of self-compassion.

*****

It took me a long time to realize how deeply judgment and self-criticism were woven into the fabric of my life. I had always passed off my self-judgment as having an immense work ethic and striving for the best—as a wife, mother, businesswoman, and woman. Perceived or self-inflected, my bar was stratospherically high. And, unintentionally, I imposed that bar on those around me.

It created a cycle of, 'It's never enough.' No amount of success or accolades could quiet my inner voice, which constantly beat out a rhythm of, 'Not enough, not enough, not enough.'

That ridiculously high bar for success started when I was very young. I became serious about becoming a classical pianist when I was nine. I was driven, focused, and deeply disciplined. While other kids were doing sports and after-school clubs, I was practicing. At nine and ten years old, I practiced at least three hours daily, which quickly matriculated to five hours a day over the next few years. By the time I was in high school, I had very little social life, and my days were completely centered around hours and hours of practice.

When you first hear about that kind of commitment and discipline, it's easy to admire it. Although I excelled in my abilities and began winning most of the competitions I entered, I never felt a tremendous sense of satisfaction. I usually dismissed my achievements as something I was expected to do, and I needed to get back to the grindstone and practice more to be ready for the next event or competition.

To be clear, no one pushed me to work that hard or to practice a mammoth number of hours.

Looking back, I understand that early childhood wounds fueled my drive. It was my way of putting salve on the wounds.

That drive, that perfectionist mentality, had served me well. I was an achiever, creating a successful business early in life. I managed children, marriage, philanthropy, and business and somehow kept all the plates spinning.

When James died, the plates stopped spinning. Striving for success, hard work, or achievements no longer mattered. Self-discipline, perfectionist achievements, or anything else I could do would not put out the fire of grief and pain.

As I began to very slowly climb out of the early stages of the most debilitating grief, I wanted to figure out what else was holding me back from healing.

As I continued to spend time in quiet meditation and prayer and began working with several profound spiritual teachers, a recurring theme kept rising to the surface, hindering my healing. It was judgment—self-judgment and the perceived judgment of others. I began to search for its underpinnings.

Truthfully, I had never tried to understand the source of self-criticism or self-attack. I had renamed it perfectionism and thought that meant I was trying to be my best self.

One of the first things I learned is that judgment often begins with fear—fear of not being accepted or fear of failure.

That made so much sense to me. I understood fear almost integrally, starting with my fear of failure as a child learning to play the piano. I feared that I wouldn't be good enough to please my teachers or parents, that I wasn't unique enough to be at the head of the pack.

It also mapped directly back to the overwhelming fear I experienced as part of my early days of grief.

Understanding fear as the root of judgment has allowed me to see judgment not as a failure but as an opportunity for healing. I've learned that a childhood wound is at the core of every judgment. It's taken me time—painful, reflective time—to trace my self-judgment back to those early wounds and understand where it all began.

*****

From people like renowned meditation teacher and psychologist Tara Brach, I've been encouraged to listen to that critical inner voice that constantly whispers judgments about myself and others, the voice that tells us we're not enough, that others aren't enough, and that life is lacking.

Working on judgment is a lot like working on shame. When you think you've rooted it out, it sneaks back in, persistent as ever. I love the analogy that judgment and shame are like mint in a garden—if not carefully contained, they'll spread wildly, taking over everything in their path. They're emotions that recur, over and over, no matter how much work we think we've done.

I find it fascinating how, when we're finally ready to face our past, life presents us with opportunities for healing.

About a year ago, I felt a pull to step back into the work world, looking for a new sense of purpose after years of struggling with grief and loss. When you're buried in work, it seems like the ultimate dream is not to work and to have time to do all the things you never get to do. But after two years of not working, I realized I needed to do something to make sense of the tragedy of the last five years. I had learned so much on my survival journey, and I wanted to share it, to let others in pain know they're not alone, and to offer hope and encouragement.

Yet, even then, judgment held me back. I was still so afraid of being judged for closing my jewelry business that I started a new venture—a podcast about survival journeys—without putting my name on it. It is called *The SoulTalks podcast*, but my name was not mentioned anywhere on the podcast or the marketing materials. I was running from judgment and social media attackers, so I initially hid behind anonymity.

One day, I was talking with a business consultant about a new opportunity that had come my way due to my podcast— the anonymous podcast. It was the first time in my life that, in a business setting, I felt paralyzed by fear. The thought of moving forward with this opportunity filled me with anxiety. The consultant, who had known me for years, began asking me questions, trying to understand why I was hesitating and seemed so uncertain. He knew the old me would have seized any opportunity without a second thought, charging ahead with confidence and determination.

As I stumbled over my words, wavering in my responses, I could feel a deep gnawing fear of being judged, failing, and not being enough to make this venture succeed. His questions began to peel back the layers, revealing the truth I had been avoiding— my fear of judgment was holding me back. It was a fear rooted in a childhood wound, a wound that whispered, *"You're not enough."*

As we continued to talk, a cool breeze of clarity swept over me, renewing my confidence. By the end of our conversation, I felt ready to pursue this opportunity, not just because of the potential success it could bring but also because doing so represented breaking free from the judgment holding me back.

I'm slowly learning that we can't live fully if we're constantly hiding from judgment. It's a journey, a lifelong one. But every step I take toward facing my fears, every bit of healing I do brings me closer to the self-compassion and joy that lies on the other side of judgment.

One of the most gracious survival tools I've learned is:

Self-compassion is the antidote to self-judgment

But the truth is that self-compassion is the only remedy for the fear of not being enough—the fear of judgment. Compassion is a balm for judgment, softening its harsh edges. When we learn to be kind to ourselves, flaws and all, we unconsciously extend that kindness to others.

Self-compassion doesn't mean excusing our mistakes or shirking responsibility— it means recognizing that we are human, that we are imperfect, and that it's okay.

I once had a friend who would say, *"It's okay not to be okay."*

****

Over the past five years, I've learned that the more compassion I show myself, the more my judgment of others softens. When we no longer feel the need to prove our worth, we no longer feel the need to judge others to elevate ourselves. We begin to see others as fellow human beings, each with their own struggles, fears, and insecurities.

A powerful practice for cultivating compassion is to imagine the inner child within each person. Beneath the surface of every adult lies a child who has experienced pain, fear, rejection, and loss. When faced with someone rude or unkind, we can remind ourselves that this person was once a vulnerable child and that their behavior may reflect their wounds and fears. This doesn't excuse hurtful behavior, but it does help us approach the situation with a more compassionate heart.

Letting go of judgment requires letting go of perfectionism, too.

For a long time, my business mantra was, *always do better, always do more.*

A few months ago, I was working with an excellent EMDR therapist, Sheri, on some of the deep-seated issues around my tendencies toward perfectionism and my fear of starting a new business.

We talked about how perfection is an illusion that is a deep-seated part of self-judgment. When we strive for perfection, we set ourselves up for failure. Perfectionism is the antithesis of self-compassion. If we flip the script and say to ourselves that perfection is not the goal, we can embrace imperfection's beauty.

Sheri began to ask me questions about my goals and dreams for the business—those were easy to answer; I wanted to help others on challenging survival journeys. I wanted to share what I had learned and lend a listening ear to those who needed it. But wrapped up in those admirable humanitarian goals was my desire to do well. For the podcast to be polished, innovative, and well-produced. You get where I'm going. I wanted to do good in the world, but I wanted it to be as perfect as possible.

After a few minutes, she asked what I liked most about doing the podcast. I told her how much I loved interviewing people, listening to their stories, and finding the edges of what made them tick.

When I stopped talking, she said, "From what you just told me, it sounds like you enjoy what's going on in the middle of the process more than creating the perfect result."

For the first time, I realized that creating the perfect, well-run, most successful business does not bring me joy. My joy comes in the unexpected, even messy parts of building a business.

We came up with a phrase for me to think about, a new business mantra, for every time I get caught up with my perfectionist thoughts:

It's Beautiful in the Middle

I now hold this phrase like a treasured amulet in my pocket. I enjoy making it my mantra because it creates space for self-compassion and exploration and erases the need for judgment.

*****

The more I sought to replace judgment with compassion, the more I noticed things shift within. I am more at peace with myself and more resilient, and my relationships have become deeper and more meaningful. I can enjoy the present moment more fully without the constant voice of judgment in my head.

In a world that often seems obsessed with judgment, where social media constantly bombards us with images of what we 'should' be, choosing a path of compassion can feel like a radical act.

I love the concept of *Radical Compassion,* a choice that can profoundly transform us. When we show ourselves compassion, we begin to view others and the world around us more compassionately.

Radical compassion is a courageous, transformative practice that challenges us to extend empathy, even in difficult situations, and make compassion the foundation of healing and connection.

Letting go of judgment in exchange for compassion allows us to become the most authentic version of ourselves.

Letting go of judgment makes room for joy to inject our lives with incredible power, resilience, and connection.

I encourage you to find compassion for yourself. Examine where you have self-doubt, self-criticism, and feel unworthy. Try to see those places through the lens of compassion—compassion for your journey, for how far you've come, and how much you've already survived. You'll be amazed at the changes you'll begin to see unfold.

Gratitude Prayer

Thank you for teaching me to extend grace to myself, even when I don't feel worthy. Thank you for this journey, on which I'm learning the healing power of compassion for myself, others, and the world.

Chapter 13

I am Enough

When I stepped back into the world of business, it was with hesitation—softly, unsure of what I truly wanted or whether I even had the confidence to run at things again. So, when my podcast began to gain attention in the healing community, I was more than surprised.

I had released around thirty episodes of The SoulTalks podcast, and what started as a passion project suddenly felt like so much more. I love every part of the process—finding people with survival stories, conducting interviews, producing, and editing.

I've owned several businesses over the years, each meaningful in their way, but none has ever felt as purposeful as this. Through my own survival journey over the last five years, I've realized that everyone is on a survival path of their own. Whether it's the loss of a loved one, betrayal, or some other deep hurt that makes it hard to even get out of bed, everyone is recovering from something.

What I've learned through these conversations is that when I give people the space to share their stories—to ask the questions that help them speak truths they might not want to say but desperately need to—it begins a healing process for them. Every guest is working through something, trying to make sense of their pain. And every time I sit down in the studio to interview someone, I am deeply humbled. The strength of the human spirit, and the immense pain we carry—it never ceases to awe me.

I constantly ask myself, "What can I contribute to this work that will truly make a difference?" Through the podcast, I've been able to craft and share my own survival tools, many of which I explore in this book. But I'm always seeking more ways to help those who are hurting, those navigating their own rocky survival journey. Because, in truth, we are all on that journey together.

Every time I question whether I am making the right moves or doing the right things in this business, something happens that validates both the work and my purpose in it. An offer to appear in a documentary titled The Frequency of Miracles, which Australian director Daniel Rechnitzer was producing in LA, arrived entirely unexpectedly.

When Daniel first approached me, I asked about the other contributors, and his response gave me pause. The list was filled with renowned experts in healing, brain research, and cutting-edge therapies, and it felt overwhelming. Of course, every ounce of me was overcome with imposter syndrome. What could I offer that would hold its weight next to such impressive qualifications?

Daniel, though, was persistent and patient. Over multiple conversations, he helped me see that sharing my personal survival journey—my experiences, tools, hard-earned hope, courage, and resilience—was just as valuable. He encouraged me to trust that my story had power, not in its perfection but in its humanity.

It took months of reflection, and I waffled more than a few times, but eventually, I realized that if my journey could offer even a spark of hope to someone on their survival journey, then I wanted to do it.

It's fascinating how life connects us with the people and ideas we need most at the perfect time. Marisa Peer is a powerful voice contributing to the documentary. She's been a therapist in the UK for thirty years, and about fifteen years ago, she developed a program called Rapid Transformational Healing. Her approach is designed to quickly uncover the root of a client's emotions and behaviors, fast-tracking their awareness and healing.

What struck me most about Marisa's work is her platform, "I Am Enough." At the heart of it are three simple yet profound words: I am enough. When I first saw those words written down, they floored me. They have the power to ground us, shift our perspective, and remind us of our inherent worth. Marisa believes that so many of our personal struggles stem from the deep-seated belief that we are not enough—whether it's not feeling smart enough, successful enough, or lovable enough. Her words resonated with parts of my life I've spent years working on.

I had recently finished writing the chapter on radical compassion, and listening to Marisa's teachings helped to expand my thoughts about self-compassion.

"I am Enough" is exactly the kind of uplifting, life-affirming message I want to share on The SoulTalks podcast. Over the last five years, I've immersed myself in self-help books, spiritual podcasts, and every bit of guidance I could find, Marisa's platform brought an added sense of clarity to my journey of growth and healing.

This morning, I was interviewed on a podcast and began talking with the host about how almost everyone runs at life from a deep-seated sense of not being enough: not having enough success or money, not being pretty enough or thin enough, not feeling loved by parents or partners. As I was talking, tears started running down the host's face, and I realized how much this resonated with her.

I wished I could have reached through the camera on my computer and hugged her.

I suspect that we often don't know what motivates us, why we work so much, or why nothing in life ever seems to fill the voids we feel—to be enough.

So many of our deeply ingrained beliefs about worth are formed in childhood and carried with us, often unchallenged. Marisa's teachings help erase those limiting beliefs and replace them with empowering ones.

One thing I've learned on my spiritual journey is that when we tell The Universe we are ready to grow and heal, God and The Universe provide a way.

As I immersed myself in Marisa's work, I was also preparing for the documentary. It turned out to be far more challenging than I expected. I had to dig deep within myself to redefine the values and beliefs that had shifted since the devasting loss of James and the journey of learning to live a life that looks so different from the one I knew.

I was incredibly grateful for the questions I was given before filming the documentary, but I was also more than a little nervous. One question made me pause: Is there something overlooked by most personal development teachings?

That question led me on a journey of reflection, considering what has been instrumental in my healing as a child and in the past five years.

Listening to Marisa, I couldn't help but think about my

114

childhood. I felt like I wasn't enough because I couldn't keep my parents from fighting, or that I wasn't lovable because loving me didn't bring them together. Looking back on my childhood, it's easy to see why I became quiet and a pleaser.

I now realize that building forts under the enormous, old grapefruit tree in the backyard or creating hideouts in the thick privacy hedges along the neighbor's fence wasn't just a way to pass the time. It was my escape. Those little hideaways became my safe places from the chaos inside our home.

One of the greatest blessings in my life was discovering music at a very young age. No one in my family was a musician or artist, but somehow, I was drawn to it—wholly mesmerized by everything musical. Classical piano, musical theater, choral groups—anything that involved music became my lifeline from the age of nine. Music wasn't just a hobby; it shaped me in ways I didn't fully understand then, but I look back on it now with deep gratitude.

Music provided me with a refuge, transforming my childhood wounds into something that validated me. Excelling at piano, singing, and performance rewired me emotionally and gave me a sense of worth and purpose.

With every performance, my confidence grew, becoming the foundation of my resilience. It helped me face life's struggles with courage.

The affirmations by my teachers gave me precisely the kind of rewiring that Marisa's teaching talks about. It didn't completely undo the feelings of not being enough or not being lovable, but it did some deep and lasting work that has stayed with me for a lifetime.

I would be remiss if I didn't acknowledge the profound

impact that teachers and mentors had on me during this time. From my first piano teacher, Vera Smith, to my last teacher after graduate school, Louise Barfield, each poured belief into me with unwavering consistency and generosity. Their faith in me laid the groundwork for much of my life. They didn't just teach me music; they taught me to believe in myself, honor my gift, and never waver in that belief. Their influence, like music, changed the course of my life.

I remember one time when I was in my early twenties, preparing to go onstage. I was about to play a big concerto I hadn't performed before, and I was nervous. I remember my teacher sitting me down and telling me that I was about to go out on that stage and give the audience an enormous gift—that I would provide them with beauty that would help heal them, help them dream bigger, and open their hearts.

I'll never forget those words. She made me realize that my playing wasn't only about me; there was significance in what I had to give in terms of the transformational power of music. That forever changed how I felt when I walked out on stage. It wasn't about how great I was as a pianist. It was about how the music I played made others feel. I had something to give that mattered.

One of the things about being involved in the arts, and I think being involved in athletics is similar, is that you realize that your gifts and abilities are unique. There has never been and never will be anyone with your exact set of skills or gifts. That understanding also underscores a deep-seated sense of worth and confidence.

By my late twenties, I had a relatively high level of confidence and resilience. I was a risk-taker, starting my own business at twenty-nine. I didn't consider failure an option. Of course, I faced my share of difficulties, but my musical training instilled in me a sense of value and worth that made me seek out opportunities and work hard to make them a success.

I lived that way until James died.

His suicide shattered my confidence. Even the most minor tasks became monumental, and grief morphed into fear. My core beliefs and sense of self were shaky for the second time in my life.

I didn't realize until he died how much of my sense of security had been tied to James. This time, confidence and resilience didn't automatically rise to fill the void.

The documentary's question made me examine the world, our influences, and what shapes us. I reflected on my early years and what had shaped me. I thought about how music had been a salvation for me, transforming my childhood wounds of insecurity into a life with a sense of worth.

Then, I had to look at the last five years and how the tragedy and trauma of James' death had shaken my core sense of self. I thought about how hard I've fought to feel a sense of worth, that I am enough even though I couldn't keep James on this earth, that I am enough to go forward and create life again, that there is a possibility of love and happiness.

As I tried to answer the question posed by Daniel, the documentary director, I could hear Marisa's teachings on repeat in my brain: about self-love and the feeling that we are enough, that we have always been enough, and that we will always be enough.

I realized how we often overlook or run past the concept of self-love in personal development teachings.

People sit in therapy chairs for years, trying to replace the love they didn't get as children. But we don't need it from one source. It's easier if you have loving parents, but you're not out of luck if you don't.

We all need praise and love. You can undo years of criticism and lack of love through self-love. The human brain doesn't know the difference.

Happy and evolved people who are successful and realize their dreams aren't the people who've been loved and praised the most from an early age. Instead, they are the people who master the art of loving themselves. It's not about arrogance or delusion. It's about confidence. It's a tool for helping you get where you want to go.

Marisa Peer's words shed new light on my survival journey. While it involved climbing out of fear, anger, and insecurity, it was also integrally laced with feelings of not being worthy of love and happiness. James' death left me feeling unlovable. As I was trying to go forward and create a new life, I didn't think I would ever be loved again or truly happy.

It took me a long time to answer the director's question, "What do you think we've missed in our pursuit of personal growth and success? Is there something overlooked by most personal development teachings?"

I answered the question by saying, "If we're to frame it up as 'what we've missed,' I would say that our definitions of success create a perfectionist mentality that results in feelings that we are not enough and are not worthy of love. We've missed choosing self-compassion over self-judgment and compassion for others instead of criticism and comparison. We've underestimated the unstoppable power of self-love."

I love those words: The unstoppable power of self-love. They have become a significant player in my survival tools.

Some of Marisa's words are so helpful in rewriting old negative self-talk and replacing it with new empowering phrases. I

now repeat these over and over during the day:
- The most important words you hear are the ones you say to yourself.
- Praise yourself for who you are as much as what you do.
- Remember, criticism withers, praise builds.

Prayer of Gratitude

I am so thankful for the gift of music and how it healed and guided me. I am deeply grateful for all of those in the healing arts who spend their lives learning and studying how to help others.

Chapter 14

Resilience, Love, and the Lessons of Jules

I t's New Year's Day 2025, and I find myself staring at a blank page, meant to begin a chapter on resilience. The irony isn't lost on me—I don't feel particularly resilient right now. Just days ago, I said goodbye to my fourteen-year-old Maltese, Jules, who had been my constant companion through the most challenging season of my life. Writing about resilience while my heart is heavy with grief feels like a cruel twist of fate.

Jules wasn't just a dog; he was a force of nature. Seven pounds of moxie, grit, and fierce protection, wrapped in a bundle of soft white fur. He carried himself like he was ten times his size, yet his heart—both literally and figuratively—was far bigger than his small frame. For fourteen years, he was my shadow, my defender, and my most loyal confidant. His love was boundless, his devotion unwavering.

In the final months of his life, Jules battled heart disease with the same tenacity that had defined him since he was a puppy. His enlarged heart pressed against his lungs, causing a persistent cough that often left him gasping for air. We did everything we could—finding the best veterinary care, managing his medication, and surrounding him with love—but his little body could only go on for so long. On December 26 we let him go, knowing it was the most compassionate choice, though it shattered our hearts.

A human and a dog's bond is like no other. It's built on loyalty, trust, and a kind of love that asks for nothing in return yet gives everything. Dogs see us in our truest form—they don't care about our titles or flaws, only how we make them feel safe and loved. When life falls apart, they stay by our side, their presence grounding us in ways we can't always explain. That's how it was with Jules. As I sit and write, resilient is the word that comes to mind—a word that perfectly describes that precious little dog. So much of my own resilience and survival is woven into the love and tenacity he brought into my life.

Grief can fracture time, dividing life into before and after. After James' death, the world felt unfamiliar; the weight of loss carved an emptiness into every corner of my life. In those early days, Jules became a bridge between the two halves of my existence. He reminded me of what remained, even when so much had been taken away.

Jules was small in stature but immense in presence. His soft, white fur and warm little body became a source of comfort when words from others fell short. He didn't ask me to explain my pain; he simply stayed. In the stillness of those quiet moments, I realized how powerful his companionship was, an unspoken reminder that even amidst devastation, I was not alone.

Each morning, Jules gave me a purpose. His needs were simple: food, water, and a walk outside. Caring for him became an anchor, pulling me out of the fog of despair. There were mornings when I didn't want to get out of bed, but his insistent bark reminded me that life, however fractured, was still moving forward. We navigated the days together, and in caring for him, I began—almost imperceptibly—to care for myself again.

Our daily walks around the neighborhood became a form of therapy. At first, they were short and perfunctory, just enough to satisfy his need for fresh air. But as weeks turned into months, those walks began to stretch longer. Jules trotted beside me, his tail wagging, always pulling hard at the leash, so excited to be outside. He would pause to sniff a flower to follow a scent trail, his enthusiasm almost yanking his leash off and pulling me out of my thoughts. Slowly, I began to see the world through his eyes—a patch of sunlight on the pavement, the rustling of leaves in the breeze, the quiet beauty of an ordinary day.

I came to understand that resilience is much like those walks with Jules. It starts small, almost imperceptibly. At first, it feels like simply going through the motions—getting out of bed, taking one step, then another. But over time, those small steps build into something greater: a quiet strength that allows us to keep moving forward, even when the path ahead feels uncertain.

I quickly realized that resilience is not a fixed trait; it's a muscle, one that grows stronger the more we use it. Much like courage, it requires practice and effort. Courage propels us to take the first step into the unknown, but resilience keeps us moving when the journey becomes difficult. Jules showed me this repeatedly, not through grand gestures but through his unwavering presence.

Jules was no ordinary dog. For all his sweetness, he had a streak of mischief that often made me laugh and frequently got him, and me in trouble. To strangers, Jules was a force to be reckoned with. At just a handful of pounds, he believed himself to be a fierce protector, a diminutive knight in shining armor. Anyone who dared get too close to me without his approval risked a sharp nip at the knees. It was his way of saying, *"This is my person. Approach at your own peril."*

I remember one afternoon at work when I was running the jewelry business, and I thought it would be nice to bring Jules along. I fantasized about the perfect little dog curled up quietly in the corner, running out and greeting customers and everyone falling in love with him. But that was not to be. Jules had other plans. When a delivery person stepped through the door, Jules sprang into action, barking furiously and circling the poor man like an intruder in a fortress. I had to apologize profusely and eventually decided that Jules was better suited to guarding me from the safety of our home.

Despite his feistiness, Jules had an unmatched capacity for love, especially for me, but also for James. In many ways, he was a bridge that helped me stay connected to James after he died. And their bond had its own poignant ending.

On the morning James took his life, he quietly slipped out of the house with Jules while I was still asleep. I often thought about what they must have exchanged that morning—a final goodbye, a silent promise of love. Knowing Jules, I'm sure he sensed something was not right, his loyal heart aware of a shift I hadn't yet realized. When I awoke, James had placed Jules just outside my bedroom door. Jules was faithfully guarding the door. James was already gone from this earth.

When the day's events unraveled, and I considered what must have been James' final moments, this was one more thing that underscored his thoughtfulness and tenderness. He had even thought to take out the dog and feed him before he took his own life. This is a heartbreaking and beautiful testament to James's love for that little dog and, truthfully, for all of us. Jules carried that memory forward in his way, reminding me of James' kindness even in tragedy.

Resilience is often described as the ability to bounce back from adversity, but I've found it to be much more than that. It's not about returning to who you were before a loss or a tragedy; it's about forging a new path forward, often with pieces of yourself that feel irrevocably broken. In the wake of James' death, resilience became my lifeline—a muscle I didn't realize I had until I was forced to use it.

At first, resilience felt impossibly far away. I didn't wake up one morning and decide to be strong; it wasn't a choice as much as a necessity. I've talked about how, in the early days of grief, survival felt like an act of defiance. Getting out of bed, brushing my teeth, and putting one foot in front of the other were small victories. I learned resilience starts with those tiny mundane acts that remind you the world hasn't stopped turning, even if it feels like yours has.

Psychologists often describe resilience as the ability to bounce back, but I think that phrase oversimplifies what resilience truly is. You don't bounce back from the loss of someone you love. Instead, you slowly, painstakingly build a new version of yourself—one that carries the scars of your pain but is also stronger for having endured it. Jules was a vital part of that process for me. His resilience—his ability to adapt, love, and protect—became a model for my resilience.

For all his quirks, Jules had an uncanny ability to be exactly what I needed, whether it was a fierce protector or a gentle comforter. On days when my grief felt like a tidal wave, he was there to pull me back to shore. His small but stubborn presence was a constant reminder that life goes on, even in the face of loss.

And he did all of that with his unique Jules flair—equal parts loving companion and tiny tyrant. Whether demanding the best spot on the couch, stealing snacks at a speed that defied logic, or barking at everything that moved, Jules was unapologetically himself.

In his quiet yet resolute way, Jules carried his grief after James' passing. For months, he found solace in the throw draped over the sofa where James had sat each evening. Every night, without fail, he would climb onto that sofa, paw at the throw until it was in just the right position, and then curl into a tight circle atop it. Jules would drag it back into place with a single-minded determination if the throw were ever moved or straightened out. It was his ritual, a way of keeping James close. Watching him do that was both gut-wrenching and profoundly comforting, a reminder that grief is universal—even our beloved pets feel its weight.

Resilience, I came to understand, is much like those nightly rituals. It's not about pushing pain away but finding ways to live alongside it. Jules wasn't pretending James hadn't gone; he was acknowledging that absence by staying connected to what he could hold onto. In his way, he showed me that resilience doesn't erase the fabric of life as we move forward.

Of course, Jules wasn't always so noble. He had a mischievous streak that kept me on my toes and sometimes made me howl laughing when I least expected to.

One day, shortly after James' passing, my son Andrew had

a particularly memorable encounter with Jules. Andrew, frustrated with Jules' incessant barking, scolded him sharply. Jules took the reprimand in stride—or so we thought. Hours later, Andrew discovered that Jules had exacted his revenge by sneaking upstairs and relieving himself all over the clothes Andrew had left on his bedroom floor. It was as if Jules was saying, "I may be small, but don't underestimate me."

Even in his defiance, Jules demonstrated a kind of resilience—a refusal to be cowed by anyone or anything. His feisty spirit reminded me that resilience isn't just about enduring hardship; it's about maintaining a sense of self, even when the word feels out of control.

In her research on grit, Angela Duckworth describes resilience as passion and perseverance in the face of long-term challenges. She writes, "Grit is living life like it's a marathon, not a sprint."

That insight resonated deeply with me. In the aftermath of James' death, resilience wasn't a burst of strength that carried me through a single moment of crisis. It was the slow, steady work of rebuilding my life piece by piece. Jules, with his daily routines and unflagging loyalty, became my partner in that marathon.

But resilience isn't always a solitary journey. I am always amazed at the collective strength that emerges in times of shared hardship, a kind of communal resilience that reminds us of our interconnectedness. In recent years, I've seen this on a global scale as communities have come together to face challenges like the COVID-19 pandemic, natural disasters, and widespread social upheaval.

Cultural resilience isn't just about surviving adversity; it's about finding meaning and purpose in the midst of it. Think of the movements for racial justice that gained momentum in 2020 or the global climate protests led by young people determined to protect the planet. These are examples of resilience as a force for change—a collective refusal to accept despair as the final word.

Resilience, I've learned, is both personal and communal. It's the strength we find within ourselves and the strength we draw from those around us. It's in the quiet courage of a dog curling up on a familiar throw. And in the loud, determined voices of people demanding justice and change. It's in how we adapt, persist, and ultimately find hope in adversity.

Even in his aging years, Jules embodied resilience. His once energetic leaps turned into careful, deliberate steps, but he never stopped moving forward. There were days when his enlarged heart kept him from running through the house at light speed or leaping up to a couch three times his size, but he'd still wag his tail and greet me with the same love and joy he'd always had. Watching him adapt to his changing body was a lesson of grace and determination—a reminder that resilience is not about denying our pain but finding a way to live alongside it.

Caring for him in the last year felt like returning the love he had given me so freely. I carried him up the stairs when his legs gave out beneath him, held him close when thunderstorms frightened him and comforted him when age brought demeaning challenges.

In his final days, Jules taught me one last lesson: that love is worth the inevitable pain of loss. Saying goodbye to him the day after Christmas felt like losing a part of myself. But even in my grief, I could feel his presence—his loyalty, his joy, his unwavering companionship.

Over the last five years, Jules has often reminded me that resilience is finding hope in a wagging tail, courage in a gentle nuzzle, and love in the simplest moments.

As I sit now in the quiet of his absence, I carry Jules with me. He's there in the lessons he taught me and the resilience he modeled for me and helped me build. His love, loyalty, and mischief taught me that life's challenges can be faced with both grace and grit. Losing him is another scar I carry, but it's also a reminder of the strength he helped me build. In his memory, I strive to embody the resilience he showed me to face each day with courage, to find joy in the small things, and to keep moving forward, one step at a time.

The memories of life with Jules will forever be etched into my heart. His love was a gift—a reminder that even in our darkest moments, there is light to be found, and even in the depths of loss, there is courage to continue.

Prayer of Gratitude

Thank you for the precious gift of Jules, who filled my life with love, loyalty, and joy. For fourteen years, he was more than a pet—he was a guardian of my heart, a source of laughter, and a quiet strength in my most difficult moments. I am profoundly grateful for the bond we shared; one built on trust, devotion, and a love that transcended words.

Chapter 15

Rewriting my Story — The Power of Thoughts

I started my first business at twenty-nine years old without an MBA, management training, or any formal background in running a company. My experience was limited to five years working for two marketing companies and a regional bank. On paper, I wasn't qualified to take such a bold leap. But I didn't see it that way.

What I did have was a lifetime of being coached by music teachers and mentors who understood the power of positive words. From an early age, my piano teachers inundated me with belief—relentlessly and consistently. They didn't only teach me how to play; they spoke to me as though I was a concert pianist in the making. Their confidence in me became the foundation for my own confidence. With every lesson, they modeled the idea that greatness begins with how you're spoken to and, more importantly, how you speak to yourself.

That belief became my guiding principle when I opened my marketing firm. People around me would say, "You're crazy to do this. Your life is going to turn into nothing but managing people." My response? "I'm looking forward to it. I love teaching people their greatness and helping them achieve it." I wasn't being flippant or overly optimistic—I genuinely meant it.

From my music coaching, I learned that words shape us. They create pathways in our minds that either hold us back or push us forward. In the same way, I had been taught to think like a pianist, I knew I could inspire others to think like leaders, creators, and innovators. For me, the joy wasn't in managing people—it was in finding what made them shine and helping them build a path to bring their best attributes forward.

But there's another side to the power of words and thoughts, one I wouldn't fully understand until after James' death.

When he died, grief became an unbearable noise in my life. It filled every space—loud, unrelenting, and all-consuming. The stories others told me about my loss reverberated in my mind: *This is so horrible. How could this happen? You'll never again have the life you had with James. This will be the hardest thing you'll ever face.* They meant well, but their words weighed me down. And I knew, deep down, that if I let those stories take root, I'd stay trapped in pain.

So, I made a choice. Just as I had learned to rewrite the narrative of my inexperience when I started my business, I decided not to let the grief write my story for me.

I wouldn't tell myself that my life was over or that survival was impossible. I wanted to find a new story that didn't deny the sorrow but gave me a path forward. It would teach me how to survive, not just by getting through each day but by creating something meaningful out of the pain.

It didn't come fast, and it didn't come easy. Healing never does. It wasn't a dramatic epiphany or a single breakthrough moment—it was baby steps—one small, shaky choice after another. But even in those early days, when grief felt like it would drown me, I understood one thing: the narrative I created in my mind would shape the reality I experienced.

I had read Louise Hay's work years before and learned how powerful our words and beliefs could be. She taught that the stories we tell ourselves shape what we believe, and what we believe becomes our life.

I decided to put that into practice. I couldn't control what had happened to me, but I could choose how I responded to it.

I started scribbling simple truths on sticky notes:

You are stronger than you think.
This is the beginning of something new.
You can survive.
There is something after this.

These weren't solutions. They didn't erase the grief or magically fix my shattered heart. But they were seeds—tiny affirmations that I planted in my mind. I stuck them everywhere: in the corners of my dressing area so I would see them when I got dressed in the morning. I tucked them into my makeup bag to get a positive jolt every time I refreshed my lip-gloss during the day. I stuck them in the middle section of my car where the gearshift was, so I had to look at them constantly while driving.

Every time I saw one of those affirmations, it was a slight nudge, a reminder that I had a choice. I could stay in the story of pain and despair or slowly start writing a new chapter. The sticky notes didn't fix everything, but they began to take root. Over time, those roots grew stronger, steadying me just enough to take the next baby step toward healing.

At first, I didn't see much change in my life, but I liked the words on my sticky notes. They gave me something to hold onto—something to think about beyond the constant pain. I made them a mantra I repeated over and over to drown out the sad narratives others were telling me: *You'll never have a good life after James. This will take your whole life to recover from.*

I refused to let those words define me. Instead, I clung to my sticky-note truths, reciting them until they became louder than the noise around me. Slowly, I began to see small shifts.

It took a few months, but I started to feel something new pulling at me. I began to want to be healthy again. I wanted food that nourished me instead of comfort food. I didn't want to sit on the sofa every night, drinking wine and drowning my sorrows.

Instead, I began moving my body again—working out harder than I had in years. Those workouts became another anchor, a reminder that I was still alive and capable of strength in my body despite my interior brokenness.

At the same time, I was still running my marketing business. On the surface, it was thriving—successful beyond what I'd dreamed of when I started my first company at twenty-nine.

I adored the people who worked for me and felt proud of what we had built together and the work we were producing. But something inside me had shifted.

James' death decimated my ideas of success as tied to achievement, material things, or accolades. The things that had once motivated me now felt hollow. The business I had been so proud of for years no longer felt fulfilling. My definitions of success were changing, and they were changing fast.

The awareness that my definitions of success were changing was both terrifying and liberating. For so long, my business had been my identity. It was the culmination of my hard work, creativity, and determination. But now it felt like I was wearing a version of myself that no longer fit.

I started to notice things I hadn't before: how drained I felt after client meetings and how little joy I got from the accolades that used to light me up. I loved the people who worked for me, but even that wasn't enough to shake the feeling that I was being called to something different—something I hadn't yet figured out.

Still, I didn't make any sudden moves. Instead, I let myself sit with the discomfort, trusting that clarity would come. In the meantime, I kept taking small steps. I poured my energy into my workouts and started eating foods that strengthened me and made me feel good. I kept leaning into positive words and ideas, letting them reshape my thoughts.

One day, as I sat at my desk, I asked myself a simple but life-altering question: *If I were to rewrite my story, my life, what would it look like?*

I didn't know the answer, but I knew it wouldn't look like the life I was living. I realized that I had been clinging to the business because it proved that I could achieve something that most people considered a remarkable lifetime achievement. But James' death had shown me that life isn't measured in accolades or success. It's measured in meaning, connection, and how alive you feel when you wake up each day.

With the support of my business mentor, I decided to close my business. It wasn't easy. But as hard as it was, it also felt like a weight lifted off me. I wasn't walking away from success—I was walking toward a new life; one I could build on my own terms.

Closing my business wasn't an easy decision; in fact, it was one of the hardest things I've ever done. For so long, it had been my identity—a reflection of everything I had worked for and achieved. Letting it go felt like I was untethering myself from everything familiar, stepping into a blank space with no map, no plan, and no guarantees.

There were moments of doubt that felt paralyzing. What if I'd made a mistake? What if I was giving up the best thing I'd ever built? But deep down, I knew I wasn't walking away from success—I was walking toward something I couldn't yet name. I wasn't just closing a chapter; I was making room for a new one, even though I had no idea what it would look like.

In the following months, I gave myself the space to explore, to ask myself what resonated with me and what I wanted my life to be. At the same time, I was learning so much about survival and grief. I noticed something that profoundly influenced me: everyone around me was carrying something—loss, pain, fear, doubt—and very few of us had space to share it, to name it, or to find a connection in it.

That realization took root inside me. It took about a year for it to grow into something I could name, but it was there, quietly but fiercely shaping the direction of my thoughts. I began to dream about creating a platform where I could share my grief and what had happened to me. More importantly, I wanted to share the survival tools I had learned.

That dream didn't come without fear. I was really anxious about stepping back into the public eye and putting myself and my story out there. What if no one cared? What if what I had to say didn't resonate with anyone?

Those questions haunted me, but I couldn't ignore the pull. I started thinking about what I could offer and realized I already had the tools to make my vision a reality.

My years as a marketer taught me how to build something from scratch and create content that connects with people. My filmmaking experience showed me the power of a good interview and how to tell someone's story in a way that feels genuine and meaningful. I wasn't starting from nothing; I had more tools and skills than I thought, and I had a heart-driven vision.

Little by little, I started to piece it together. It wasn't polished or perfect, but it was real. As I leaned into the idea, I realized I wanted to create a space where people could connect—not just with my story but with their own. A place where they could feel less alone in their struggles and maybe even find the tools to move forward. I wanted to have the conversations no one seemed to be having, the ones that spoke to the hidden parts of our pain.

The first steps were messy and imperfect. I sketched out ideas for a podcast, brainstorming topics, and potential guests. Then, I dusted off my production skills and reconnected with my favorite people in the production business to help me record and edit the episodes.

I was so nervous during the first round of interviews we filmed. I questioned everything—whether I was ready, whether I could open up the emotional space on camera for other people to feel comfortable telling their stories, and whether this would even work. But alongside the nerves, there was a surprising sense of peace, as if something inside me knew I was exactly where I needed to be. Crafting questions that allowed others to uncover and share their stories didn't feel like a job—it felt like a calling.

Then came a moment I didn't expect. During one interview, the guest turned the questions back on me, asking about my own pain and my journey after losing James. I tried to hold it together, but the floodgates opened, and I cried like a baby—on camera, in front of the crew, and in front of the world of social media.

I felt 180 degrees removed from the woman I had once been—the one who led a successful business with precision and polish but who never let down her guard. This was different. It was unfiltered and vulnerable in a way I'd never allowed myself to be before. For the first time since James died, I realized that vulnerability wasn't a weakness—it was a bridge.

As I started recording episodes, something unexpected happened. The conversations I had—with myself and others—began to transform me. Sharing my story out loud, hearing others share theirs, and seeing firsthand how we are all connected in our struggles became a healing I hadn't expected.

And people started listening. They didn't just listen; they reached out. They told me how much they related, how much they needed a space like this, and how hearing these stories made them feel seen and less alone. Every message and every comment reminded me that this work mattered, not just to me but to so many others navigating their struggles.

The first time I had an episode go viral, I could hardly believe it. I danced around the house like a kid, laughing for joy. For an entire week, I felt a sense of celebration I hadn't felt in years—not because of the numbers or the attention but because it confirmed what I had hoped from the beginning: that people were craving connection, honesty, and a space to share their stories.

Since the first week I started the podcast, every week, someone who has survived the suicide of a loved one has reached out and asked, "I just lost my husband, how do I get through this week? Can you give me some tools? Or "My daughter took her life last week; I don't know how to go on; how did you do it?"

These gut-wrenching questions and the human pain they express have validated why I stepped out of my shell and returned to the public eye again. The need for help, and for someone who's been there, has helped me make sense of what happened to James, me, and my boys.

In every story I've shared, I hear a piece of my journey reflected back to me. These stories lift me up and challenge me to dig deeper to find more tools to help others survive.

None of this transformation has been tidy. It has been messy, painful, and full of moments when I wanted to give up. However, the podcast and these incredible people willing to share their stories have taught me that the mess is where healing happens, and that vulnerability is the soil where growth takes root.

I am beginning to see my own transformation more clearly. The sticky note mantras that carried me through those early days of grief and sorrow were foundational for me. Looking back, I can see how powerful they were as survival tools. They helped me shape my thoughts and, ultimately, my entire life forward.

For all the business success I've experienced in the past, nothing compares to the sense of purpose I feel with this platform about survival. Building companies, achieving milestones, and earning accolades once defined what I thought fulfillment looked like. But this work—creating a space for people to share their stories and discover their strengths is different. It's as if every step of my life, every success, and every heartbreak has led me to this moment.

What started as a personal journey has grown into something much bigger. It isn't about my story anymore—it is a shared space for survival, healing, and hope.

Prayer of Gratitude

Thank you for the gift of transformation, for the power of our thoughts and minds to help us heal and lead us into the next phases of our lives. Thank you for the resilience and grace to rewrite my story with hope and purpose.

Epilogue

Love Remains

In the years since James' death, I have worked diligently to rebuild my life, anchoring myself in the things that give me life. But healing has not been a straight line. It has been jagged, cruel, and disorienting.

I have stumbled more times than I can count, making choices I never would have made before—the kinds of choices that only grief and loneliness can justify. I have let the wrong people in because vulnerability blurred my judgment. I have made financial and life decisions that, in hindsight, weren't in my best interest because loss has a way of silencing the instincts that once protected you.

One of the hardest places to face after a long and happy marriage is the question that echoes in the silence, will there ever be love again? Will I always be alone? Will I always eat by myself, go to sleep by myself, and wake up to an empty bed? Will I ever be held again?

Loneliness is more than an ache; it's like an erosion. It wears you down in ways you don't see until you're hollow. It is an economist of suffering, tallying every loss, every moment that will never be shared again. Loneliness is a ruthless companion; invading space you never thought it could reach. It is not about a lack of resilience or failing to practice gratitude or lacking spiritual discipline. It is a force that leaves you breathless and untethered.

It is the realization that the one person who carried your most vulnerable truths—who knew every unspoken thought, every quiet fear, every unsaid dream—is gone. It is the crushing weight of knowing that the only other person who loves your children with the same biological instinctive ferocity is no longer here. It is sitting in a room full of people, laughing at the right moments, saying all the right things, and yet feeling like you are screaming silently because no one in that room carries your shared history. No one else remembers the little things that made up the language of your marriage, the inside jokes, the shorthand glances, the effortless understanding.

And then there are the nights. The nights when grief is not just a visitor but a suffocating presence. The nights when you reach for someone who is no longer there.

I didn't want anyone but James. But I also didn't want to be alone. It's a strange and unbearable contradiction.

Two years after James' death, I stepped into another relationship. It was a fragile, complicated thing—two wounded people trying to create something new from the wreckage of loss. His loss came from the deep betrayal of divorce, mine from the deep betrayal of suicide. We had moments of great fun and joy, moments when I thought maybe, just maybe, I had found my way back to something resembling home. But grief and love are strange bedfellows; ultimately, we could not bridge the distance that loss had carved between us.

So here I am, at the five-year mark of James' death. Once again, I find myself standing at the beginning, learning what it means to start over when you never wanted to begin again.

Friendship is one of the purest, most generous forms of love. It is love without obligation, without the weight of vows or legal ties—just the simple, beautiful choice to walk alongside someone, no matter how broken, lost, or weary they might be. My friends have done this for me over and over again, and in their presence, I have relearned what it means to be healthy, even when my world feels like it's unraveling.

My circle of friends, these remarkable soul-nourishing people—have taught me that healing is not a solitary journey. Every time I have collapsed under the weight of loss, they have been there, lifting me up and reminding me of my resilience when I could not see it for myself. They have held space for my pain, but they have also reintroduced me to joy, laughter, and the simple sacred act of being present in the now.

One of the hardest lessons I have learned is that not all friendships survive grief. Loss reshapes you, and in that reshaping, some relationships fall away. There are those who could not sit in my sorrow, wanted me to be 'better' faster, and mistook my sadness for weakness. Some disappeared when my grief became inconvenient, and they could not understand why I was not the same person I had been before James died.

But then there are the ones who stayed, the ones who did not need me to be anything other than exactly who I was at each moment. The ones who reminded me that I am still whole, still worthy, still capable of extraordinary love and extraordinary joy.

And then, there are the remarkable gifts of new friendships unexpectedly and profoundly life-giving. One of the sweetest, purest friendships in my life is Christa. She has walked me through three years of tears, hurt, and pain, never wavering in her belief in me. She has built me up when I felt like I was falling apart, seeing the best in me even when I couldn't see it myself. She has helped me walk out of my grief, not by forcing me to move faster than I was ready, but by standing beside me, holding space for my healing. Christa is one of those rare, irreplaceable gifts—proof that even in the wake of loss, life has a way of bringing us exactly who we need.

Love—true love—is never one-sided. It is a constant exchange, a rhythm of giving and receiving. My friends and family have given me so much, and in their presence, I have learned the power of reciprocity. To show up, listen, and be present for them just as they have been for me.

I used to think James was the only person who truly saw me, who understood me at my deepest level. But grief has a way of revealing unexpected truths. And the truth is, love is abundant. It does not exist in only one person or in only one kind of relationship. Love is in the friendships and family that sustain me. It is in the voices that remind me, again and again, that I am not alone.

And so, as I stand once more at the threshold of an uncertain future, stepping out alone yet again, I do not do so without love. I do not do so without the tattoos on my soul of every person who has walked this path with me.

For a long time, I thought my life had been shattered beyond repair. That nothing could exist beyond the grief, beyond the unbearable ache of losing James. And in many ways, that loss will always live within me. There will always be a space in my heart that belongs only to him.

But grief, as I have learned, is not the end of the story.

In the midst of my sorrow, in the wreckage of what was, something else has taken root. Something steady, unwavering. Something that has carried me when I could not carry myself. Love did not end when James died. It transformed. It became the hands of my sister reaching for me in my darkest moments. It became the arms of my children wrapping around me repeatedly, grounding me in the fierce, unbreakable bond we share. It became my friends' unwavering presence, showing up to remind me that I am not alone.

Beyond the hands and hearts that have carried me, there has also been an infinite source of love and strength holding me through it all. My faith has been an anchor, reminding me that even in the darkest moments, I am never truly alone. God— The divine, the great supplier of all things—has been ever-present, weaving grace into my story, sustaining me when I had nothing left to give. There is a sacredness in knowing that love is not just found in the people around me but is also an unshakable presence within me, guiding me forward and reminding me that I am deeply held, deeply known, and never forsaken.

This is the foundation upon which I am building my life forward. Not on loss, not on loneliness, but on the people who have stood beside me, who have given me the strength to rise again.

There is a tenderness in rebuilding—a slow, deliberate choice of what to carry with me and what to leave behind. It is learning to live inside my own skin again, to trust myself again.

For so long, I was afraid of what the future might hold. I was afraid that I would never feel the same depth of love and connection again. However, the most profound lesson I have learned is that love does not exist in only one form. It is not limited to the shape of a marriage or the structure of the life I once knew.

Love is expansive.

I do not know exactly what comes next. But I know this: I am not alone.

And maybe that is enough.

Acknowledgments

This book would not exist without the unwavering support, gentle nudges, sense of humor, and shared tears of Cheryl Benton, my incredible editor and publisher. Cheryl, your belief in me and this book has meant more than I can express. Thank you for your wisdom, your kindness, and the love you pour into everything you do.

I have been carried, held, and lifted by so many remarkable people during these past five years of survival and transformation. Many of you are woven into these pages, and your presence is a testament to the power of love and friendship. To my sister, Lisa, and my niece, nephew, and aunt—Missy, John Michael, and Darlene. To my precious friends Marie, Princess, Laura, Tracy, Les, Peter, Scott, Carrie, Amy, Shirley, Adi, Sandra, Christa, Drew, Lisa, and Mert—you have breathed life into me when I felt hollow, given me space to grieve, and helped me find my way back to joy. I can count on you day and night; for that, no words are big enough to thank you.

With all my love and deepest gratitude---thank you for walking this path with me.

~*Theresa*

About the Author

Theresa Bruno is a writer, speaker, coach, and host of The SoulTalks podcast. She is a trained classical pianist and a successful entrepreneur who helmed a regional marketing firm in the Southeast and created a high-end jewelry line with a celebrity following. Since the death of her husband, James, she has dedicated her life to helping others navigate their survival and loss.

Appendix

Survival Tools • Resources

Survival Tools

Grief, loss, and rebuilding a life after devastation can feel impossible, like navigating an unfamiliar world without a map.

Throughout this book, I have shared the rawest parts of my journey—the heartbreak, the loneliness, the moments of despair——but also the resilience, the healing, and the profound love that has carried me forward.

Along the way, I have learned that survival is not just about enduring pain---it is about finding the tools that help you keep going, the lifelines that pull you forward when you feel like you have nothing left.

In this book, I have shared the practices, perspectives, and truths that have helped me rebuild my life after loss. This addendum is a collection of those survival tools---practical, emotional, and spiritual resources that have carried me through my darkest moments.

I hope that no matter where you are on your own journey, you will find something here that meets you where you are, offering you strength, clarity, and the reminder that you are never truly alone.

Chapter Two

Understanding that the process of Grief is a long one.

Grief is not something you overcome. It's not something you fight. It's an emotion you get to know.

*****

Chapter Three

Prayer is a Lifeline.

Whether you call it God, The Universe, or a Divine Consciousness, lean into the God of your understanding. Miracles, big and small, will find their way to you, and you will find the strength to hold on.

*****

Chapter Four

Gratitude.

Each moment of gratitude was pulled from the depths of my sorrow, and I clung to it with fierce determination. It forced me to confront the broken pieces of my world and find meaning in the chaos. Gratitude was not a quiet reflection—it was a fierce act of rebellion against the consuming grief.

*****

Chapter Five

Nature Can Help Bear Our Pain.

When we find ourselves in pain—whether from loss, betrayal, heartache--- the burdens of life—it is nature that so often calls us back to ourselves. Nature reminds us that we are part of something greater that moves with us, embraces us, and holds us when we feel we cannot carry our pain.

*****

Chapter Six

Feeling Judged Lights a Match to Shame.

I gradually realized that the shame I carried from the business failure made recovering from the overwhelming sorrow of losing James even harder.

*****

Chapter Seven

Sharing Our Pain Lessens Its Power.

Find your own 'Kitchen Table' of family and friends who will journey with you, champion you, and hold you up when you don't have the strength to carry the weight of your own life. They don't have to have answers. The healing comes in sharing your pain.

*****

Chapter Eight

Letting Go Doesn't Mean Forgetting Them.

Letting go means finding a way to honor their lives while understanding that we couldn't carry their pain for them. It means embracing our own healing, step by step, even when it feels impossible.

*****

Chapter Nine

Acceptance Became My Bridge.

I began to focus on what I could do with the life I had now. I started asking myself questions that felt daunting at first: What do I want for my life moving forward? What kind of person do I want to become through this? How can I find meaning in this pain?

*****

Chapter Ten

Our family didn't end with James' death.

Jordan and Andrew taught me that love can be redefined. We will never be the same family we were before, but we can become something else—something equally as strong, loving, and, I think, more resilient.

*****

Chapter Eleven

I Will Rise.

I was tiptoeing into a new life, tracing the edges of what could come next and beginning to understand just how necessary it was to be gentle with myself.

Sometimes, I went backwards, swallowed up by the shadows of my perceived failures, wounds, and fears of never moving beyond the past. Gradually, however, I began to believe that loss alone did not define my life.

*****

Chapter Twelve

Self-Compassion is the Antidote to Self-Judgment.

The truth is that self-compassion is the only remedy for the fear of not being enough—the fear of judgment. Compassion is a balm for judgment, softening its harsh edges. When we learn to be kind to ourselves, flaws and all, we unconsciously extend that kindness to others.

*****

Chapter Thirteen

I Am Enough.

The core idea is that when we truly internalize the belief that we are enough, just as we are, without needing to prove ourselves or seek validation, we begin to trust in our own worth and potential. This leads to a rise in confidence and resilience and a fearless pursuit of our goals, free from the fear of failure or rejection.

*****

Chapter Fourteen

Resilience is a muscle, one that grows stronger the more we use it.

Like courage, resilience requires practice and effort. Courage propels us to take the first step into the unknown, but resilience keeps us moving when the journey becomes difficult.

*****

Chapter Fifteen

Your Thoughts Create Your Life.

I learned that words shape us. They create pathways in our minds that either hold us back or push us forward. The stories we tell ourselves shape what we believe, and what we believe becomes our life.

I decided to put that into practice. I couldn't control what had happened to me, but I could choose how I responded to it.

*****

Resources

None of us walk this journey alone. Along the way, I have been shaped and guided by the wisdom of those who came before me—thinkers, writers, psychologists, poets, and spiritual teachers whose words tethered me to their wisdom and strength. Their insights have illuminated my path, challenged my perspectives, and helped me make sense of the unimaginable.

This addendum is a tribute to them—a collection of the voices that have influenced my healing and growth. I hope that just as their words have supported me, they may also serve as a source of inspiration, comfort, and guidance for you as you navigate your own journey.

Julia Samuel, Grief Psychotherapist
"… grief unmasks our greatest fears, strips away our layers of protection, and reveals our innermost selves."

C.S. Lewis, Author, Theologian, A Grief Observed
"No one ever told me that grief felt so like fear."

Tracy L. Clark, Pastor, Author, God Where Are You? It's Me!
"Your connection to God is your most sacred connection. It is the one that will lead you back to the healing of your spirit. It is the one that will allow you to open your intuition and break free of fear."

Robert Emmons, Psychologist, Author, Thanks! How the new Science of Gratitude can make you Happier
"Gratitude is the ability to affirm the good in life even while facing hardship. Gratitude doesn't minimize pain; it places it in context. It lets us say, Yes, this hurts—but there's still beauty here."

Mary Oliver, Poet, Wild Geese

Pema Chodron, Author, When Things Fall Apart

Brene Brown, Author, Daring Greatly
"…three things keep you from the path of healing: secrecy, shame, and judgment."

Lisa Zimmer, Spiritual Guide
"Spirit Whispers"

Henri Nouwen, Author, Theologian
"When we honestly ask ourselves which person in our lives means the most to us, we often find that it is those who, instead of giving advice, solutions, or cures, have chosen rather to share our pain and touch our wounds with a warm and tender hand."

Anne Rolphe, Author, Epistles: A Memoir of Grief
"Grief is in two parts. The first is loss. The second is the remaking of life."

Viktor Frankl, Author, On Finding Meaning Amid Suffering
"In some ways, suffering ceases to be suffering at the moment it finds a meaning, such as the meaning of a sacrifice."

Ranier Maria Rilke, Author, Letter to a Young Poet
The point is to live everything. Live the questions now. Perhaps then, someday, far in the future, you will gradually, without noticing it, live your way into the answers.

Maya Angelou, Poet, Author, When the Caged Bird Sings
She always reminded her readers to take time to sit back and celebrate themselves in the growth process.

Gabby Bernstein, Author, The Judgment Detox

In compassion, we can choose again—love over fear, connection over separation, compassion over criticism.

Marissa Peer, Rapid Transformational Therapist, Author, I Am Enough

We all need praise and love. You can undo years of criticism and lack of love through self-love. The human brain doesn't know the difference.

Happy and evolved people who are successful and realize their dreams aren't the people who've been loved and praised the most from an early age. Instead, they are the people who master the art of loving themselves. It's not about arrogance or delusion. It's about confidence. It's a tool for helping you get where you want to go.

Angela Duckworth, Psychologist, Researcher on Grit

"Grit is living life like it's a marathon, not a sprint."

www.ingramcontent.com/pod-product-compliance
Lightning Source LLC
Chambersburg PA
CBHW060139150626
46550CB00015B/2057